I COULD
OF YOUR
LOVE FOREVER

delirious? d:

Regal

From Gospel Light
Ventura, California, U.S.A.

Regal Books
From Gospel Light
Ventura, California, U.S.A.
Printed in China
www.regalbooks.com

All Scripture quotations, unless otherwise indicated, are taken from the *Holy Bible, New International Version*®. Copyright © 1973, 1978, 1984 by International Bible Society. Used by permission of Zondervan Publishing House. All rights reserved.

Cover Design by Stewart John Smith
Interior Design by JoshuaTalbotDesign.com

Other versions used are
THE MESSAGE—Scripture taken from *THE MESSAGE.* Copyright © by Eugene H. Peterson, 1993, 1994, 1995. Used by permission of NavPress Publishing Group.
NASB—Scripture taken from the *New American Standard Bible,* © 1960, 1962, 1963, 1968, 1971, 1972, 1973, 1975, 1977, 1995 by The Lockman Foundation. Used by permission.

Library of Congress Cataloging-in-Publication Data
Delirious? (Musical group)
 I could sing of your love forever / Delirious?
  p. cm.
 ISBN 0-8307-4302-2 (trade paper)
 1. Contemporary Christian musicians—England—Biography. 2. Contemporary Christian musicians—
Religious life. I. Title.
ML421.D45I2 2007
 782.25—dc22

                                                                                              2006037798

Contents

Foreword

Matt Redman

In the year 1779, John Wesley introduced a new hymn book, hoping that these songs would become in the worshiper "a means of raising or quickening the spirit of devotion; of confirming his faith; of enlivening his hope; and of kindling and increasing his love for God." Our worship songs are for *Jesus*—yet as they work their way out of our hearts and toward heaven, they so often work wonders in *us*. The songs of Delirious? are a fantastic example of this—through them and their songs, countless people around the world have experienced just what Wesley was describing over 200 years ago: strengthened faith, renewed hope and a heightened sense of love and devotion to their God. These are the things a great worship song does.

At the time of the very first Delirious? worship songs (or "Cutting Edge" as they were known back then), I was privileged to be working in the studio with Martin Smith as my producer. One of the perks was that I got a preview of what was brewing in the Delirious? teapot. I remember smiling from ear to ear the first time I heard "The Happy Song," and weeping tears of intercession the first time I heard "Did You Feel the Mountains Tremble?"

Hearing the songs on a CD was powerful enough, but as I started to lead these songs at various youth gatherings around the UK, I saw a whole different dynamic kick in. It was amazing to see these young worshipers connecting with such a fresh expression of praise—it was as if they'd finally found their voice in worship. Not surprisingly, the songs started to sweep the nation—you literally couldn't go to a youth worship meeting in the UK without singing at least one Delirious? song. Before long, their music began to journey across the ocean, and to this day Delirious? songs inspire worshipers on every continent of the globe.

And while Delirious? has gone global, they haven't lost their local roots. On the average Sunday morning, if you go back to the school where those very first Cutting Edge worship meetings were held, you'll find Martin, John, Stew, Tim and Stu G. They might be leading up the front or perhaps sitting with the rest of the congregation—but they are *being* church. And perhaps that's why the songs keep flowing. The reason these guys can sound *The Mission Bell* with both integrity and passion is that they've been right there all along. Their feet have touched the soil of South America, Africa, Australia, India, Eastern Europe and the United States—yet all the while they're still placed firmly on the ground in the lesser known land of Littlehampton, living and praying to see the kingdom of God come.

Doubtless there'll be many more exciting new songs and sounds from the band in the future. But for now, read these stories behind the past ones—and celebrate all that God has chosen to do through them.

Matt Redman

Foreword

Darlene Zschech

I still remember where I was the first time I heard a Delirious? CD. I was doing some ironing (okay, some things in life never change) and to make the chore bearable, I put on one of the CDs I'd been sent to have a listen to. You know that feeling when you hope a CD is great but often it's not quite what you were expecting? Well, this time I was so surprised—there was an electricity in what I was hearing, and these guitar sounds started to suggest that I listen more closely. The words started to flow, and my heart started to lean in to the passionate and prophetic nature of what was being sung over me.

For the first time, I felt like someone was actually describing what my heart had always longed to say. Whenever I had been songwriting, I always seemed to choke on the more intimate lyrics—I knew at that moment that my own journey of healing and understanding in worship still had a ways to go.

So here it was, Cutting Edge, 1, 2 ,3, 4, and I couldn't get enough. The songs were brave, raw, honest—these writers were not afraid to admit their imperfections. Their music was freeing, even as it challenged me to open up the deep places of my life to the hand of God.

But do you think I could get hold of a Delirious? album here in Australia? No! So every time we traveled, I would bring home as much of their music as my cheap and somewhat unstable suitcases would allow (the airlines were a bit more flexible on weight limits back then!), and I would give a CD to everyone I could. These songs became very much a part of the soundtrack to my journey in Christ—and "History Maker" was the one that became my heart's theme song.

Not surprisingly, the first time I met the guys in the United States I was actually wearing a Delirious? T-shirt, which made me look like a crazy woman, but, hey, they had made a profound impression on my heart. And their influence continues to gather great momentum, as just last year I sent Martin a text from the middle of East Africa, where Mark and I were working with Compassion International, to let him know that here we were in Rwanda, and hundreds of orphans were singing "I Could Sing of Your Love Forever." The power of a great song is truly breathtaking.

Over the years, Mark, myself and our daughters have had the great privilege to share platforms with them, to share holidays, new songs, laughter, meals, mountaintop experiences and some valleys. We count them among some of our closest friends, and we will be eternally grateful to God for the gift that they are.

The songs continue to come ("Our God Reigns" is a must-listen!), the revelation continues to be unveiled, their leadership choices continue to be inspired and brave, their families continue to flourish in faith and in numbers, and the message of these songs continues to confront any mediocrity that might be tempted to settle in to the secret places of our hearts.

Thanks, Delirious? Thanks for staying on course and paying the price, and thanks for the countless hours of leading so many of us into the glorious courts of our King. I personally am ever grateful.

From my heart,

Darlene Zschech

P.S. I don't think that ironing ever did get done!

Introduction

It's an age-old question: Where does inspiration come from? Is it merely chance when a melody arrives out of nowhere, picks an individual to land on and channels itself down a pen onto paper?

The Rolling Stones' Keith Richards's opinion is that you just stick your "antenna" in the air and catch what's floating around in the atmosphere. In a way, we can't disagree with that philosophy, since both Stu and I recall moments of pure inspiration when we didn't dare visit the restroom for fear of missing something or stepping out of "the artistic zone."

But there is another side to it, and it's the issue of *craft*. This may surprise people, but songwriting is hard work. Hours are spent pouring over notebooks, scraps of paper, napkins, Dictaphone recordings and rhyming dictionaries. Songs get thrown out, re-written, sped up, slowed down and the chorus of one swapped with the verse of another.

Whether it's inspiration or perspiration, all art is created out of life. The songwriter's life is one big sponge for all he sees and hears, and it's out of this sponge that we squeeze our songs and what we have to say. This book is a window into the lives behind our songs. It's a glimpse of the celebration and struggle of living life with God.

We hope you'll enjoy these stories of our journey so far and the songs along the way. Thanks for singing them over the years and letting them be a part of the soundtrack of your life. We are honored and always will be.

Happy reading,

Martin and Stu

I Could Sing of
Your Love
Forever

Martin Smith

Summertime is always fantastic, and my memory of the one in 1993 was extra special, as I'd been dating Anna for about six months and love was in the air!

I'd been invited to spend a week on holiday with her family in Devon (southwest England) in a big old house on a wooded hillside towering over a beautiful estuary below. My roommate for the week was Jon (Anna's younger brother), who was only 17 then, who revealed to me the art of sleeping past one o'clock in the afternoon. Jon still can beat anyone hands down for the hibernation award.

One afternoon I decided to climb the hill behind the house to take in this beautiful scenery. Sometimes in life you are aware of time slowing to the point that it feels like it stands still, and I was in one of these moments. I just became aware of the awesomeness of God and the brilliance of His creation, surrounded as I was by incredible beauty, rolling hills and rivers running to the sea.

Over the mountains and the sea, your river runs with love for me just came to me and the rest of the song appeared in an instant—like it had fallen out of the sky. (I don't recall this ever happening—most of the songs take a few months to fashion into something presentable.) *I could sing of your love forever* became the chorus over the same chords as an expression of how amazing it is to know and experience the love of God.

After writing that song, I remember packing up my guitar and lyric book and heading back to the house to see everyone. Sarah (Anna's older sister who married Stew, our drummer) offered me a cup of tea and asked to hear the new idea. I played it through, and she thought it was nice but nothing extraordinary.

People have often asked over the years what it feels like to write a song that travels the world and becomes a modern-day hymn. Well, at the time you're completely unaware of the journey a song will take—and that's a good thing, otherwise you would force it into something tarnished by commercialism instead of a genuine offering to God and a genuine piece of art. The only excitement you have initially is when you introduce your song to the church and hope it connects with the congregation so that they can use it as their own prayer.

They say that one song can change your life, and I guess this was the song that did. For us as a band, this song opened up doors in countries we'd never heard of before and allowed the Church at large to own what Delirious? was doing, playing God music inside and outside the Church. It wasn't necessarily the coolest song in the world—but it was a simple prayer of love to Jesus.

It's crazy when I hear my songs being sung by other artists and in the most amazing circumstances. I once turned on the TV to see Michael W. Smith playing the song in front of the U.S. president at a state function. I was changing my youngest daughter's diaper at the time and thought, *What a strange life this is!* I've been on a train when someone's phone goes off and the ring tone is "I Could Sing"—it makes me feel grateful, proud and weird all at the same time!

In general, people think you're a better or more spiritual person for writing these songs, but songwriting is a gift. These worship songs are the work of the grace of God. I have the privilege of knowing some of the great writers of our generation, and they all have the same sense of vulnerability and introspection, both of which are needed for being creative and giving a voice to the Church. But these same traits can bring a selfishness and, at times, mood swings that make songwriters difficult for their partners and friends to be around. To be creative you have to live in your own head, and at times I'm sorry and embarrassed at the way I can shut out my wife and children. It's a balance, and sure there's grace, but the great songs demand great lives to back them up. No, we are not better people, not any better or closer to God than anybody else—we simply have a gift to bring songs that the average believer feels he or she could have written.

Jesus' first commandment was that we love the Lord our God with all our heart, with all our soul, with all our mind and with all our strength (see Mark 12). This passage defines us as Christians and is the essence of all that we are and all we can do. To love and worship God is what we're made for—and salvation is a complete rebirth, like going from black and white to color, from mono to surround sound, from economy to first class! (If there's anyone at British Airways that could help, then let us know!) "For God so loved the world" includes you and me—and if that doesn't get us *dancing with joy*, as the song says, then nothing will!

There will come a point when we won't need these songs anymore. One day we'll be standing face to face with Jesus, our great Lord and Savior, and each of us will have our own custom-made song of thanks that will explode from within. God, we will live with You for eternity and *sing of Your love forever*.

I Could Sing of
Your Love
Forever

2

this lonliness
is temporary...

Heaven

Stu G

I'm glad I'm not flying today!

I'm watching breaking news regarding how British security services have disrupted a plot to blow up planes mid-flight. Twenty-four people have been detained in connection with the bombing attempt, and the airports are in chaos. I'm *so* glad I'm not flying today!

This news inspired me to write about the song "Heaven." But the story behind the song "Heaven" actually starts with another song—"White Ribbon Day." Growing up in the seventies, I feel like I've known nothing but tension and violence in Northern Ireland. The recent troubles burst onto the world's headlines in 1969 when the British Army were deployed to help control riots and violence on the streets. The root cause of it all was a potent mixture of civil rights and struggle for political control, which went back for centuries.

Most people in the UK were affected some how, and I wasn't without my own sad experiences. In the eighties I lost a school friend who had joined the army and gotten blown up by an IRA bomb. I had another friend who worked at Harrods when an IRA bomb was detonated in the store. A few years later I was sitting in my lounge on the Hornsey Road in North London when the whole house shook with the explosion that destroyed the Bishopsgate in the financial heart of the city a few miles away. Then in March 1994, while I was taking an electrical testing class at a hotel near Heathrow Airport, the IRA drove a truck into the car park and launched mortars onto the runway!

Terrorists or freedom fighters?

All I know is that lives were wasted and people lived in fear. Both Republicans and Loyalists caused terrible atrocities. It is a difficult issue—and I don't profess to know a lot; in fact, I feel like I know nothing. But I know a man who does!

Enter Simon Trundle. Simon is currently a pastor of a church in Northamp-tonshire—but he leads a double life. He is a counterterrorism consultant to governments and large corporate institutions. An expert on ballistics and security, he travels the world advising governments in various trouble hotspots, and he is manager of the UK commercial blast trials program.

His work colleagues lovingly call him Pastor Blaster!

Whilst living in Northern Ireland, his company designed and built the security defenses for the military barracks and police stations. The Trundle family lived and worked in Belfast and because of his job, Simon himself was a target of the IRA. In fact, his friend was murdered while driving Simon's car, a case of mistaken identity—a tragic event that affected Simon deeply. Simon survived three separate attempts on his life, and it was during this time that he found his faith.

We met Simon in 1996 at a gig in Bedfordshire. Martin had written "White Ribbon Day," after watching a news article about the marches for peace in Northern Ireland at which everyone wore white ribbons. We put the song in the set that night, and it impacted Simon so much he met us afterward and said, "That song must get released as a single!" He promptly gave us money to get the ball rolling. Andy Piercy helped us with production and knew a guy called Tony Patoto at Total Records in London. It was the beginning of our journey into the singles market—and also the beginning of a beautiful friendship with Tony P.

"White Ribbon Day" made it to number 41, a little disappointing but something to build on. We couldn't wait to play in Ireland, and sure enough the invitations started to come in. I can't remember much about our first gigs there, but what I do remember are places and people.

Simon very kindly took on the role of driver and tour manager—thankfully he didn't tell us he was checking for explosive devices every morning before we set off, as he was still a target! But his knowledge of the history of Ireland was fascinating. Every road we turned down seemed to have its own story. Large murals on houses, curbstones painted with the colors of either the union flag or the flag of the Irish Republic, army checkpoints at shopping centers, a single army helicopter hovering all day above the Falls Road—a place I'll never forget.

As we walked and drove down the Falls Road—which is the main road through West Belfast, synonymous with the troubles—we could literally feel the struggle. It was in the air we breathed and on the pavements we walked on. Tension, pain, injustice, violence and pride were staring us in the face.

I started to reflect out loud about the fact that only God is everywhere at once and that the devil as a created being can only be in one place at a time. I said, "You know, today it felt like we walked down a road where the devil's been."

Martin said, "Sounds like a song!" and we began to talk about the contrast of living through the struggle, doing the best we can, while knowing that one day it will all be over and God will wipe every tear from our eye (see Isa. 25:8; Rev. 7:17). *Heaven is my home and there'll be no shame to bear.* It sounds like such a quick fix thing to say: "Don't worry, one day it'll all be over!" Although it's true, I don't mean it like that at all.

We've been to several countries around the world where the people have suffered terribly—Rwanda, Croatia, South Africa and of course Northern Ireland, to name a few. The same feeling exists in all those places: the same taste in the air, the same spirit of fear, and the same history of atrocities committed while governments turned a blind eye. Our friend Simon says the first casualty of war is the truth; the second is civilians—ordinary, everyday human beings like you and me, who hurt and bleed and die.

Children have seen their own parents blown up, shot or hacked to death in front of their eyes. Glib phrases and clichés do not work in these places. *The kids have seen things they should never have seen.* So, yes—one day it will all be over, but I don't subscribe to the "I'm a Christian; get me out of here!" way of thinking. We have no choice but to be here now—this is our time! This is our life to live! This is our chance to make a difference.

Jesus teaches us to pray, "Your kingdom come, Your will be done, on earth as it is in heaven." It's through our lives that heaven can come to Earth. Two thousand years ago, 12 followers of Jesus turned the world upside down . . . how much more could all of us do today?

Did You Feel the Mountains Tremble?

the Mountains

Tremble?

Martin Smith

It was January 1994 and Tim, Stew and I were playing at an event called Pioneer South. It was a chance for all the local churches along the south coast of England to get together and have a big night of teaching and worship. The venue was an old, rundown cabaret hall on the site of a holiday camp in Bognor Regis, complete with spinning stage and red velvet curtains.

That night, as I stood at the front leading a thousand people as they sang their hearts out to God, a man stepped out of the shadows. He took the microphone, stared me straight in the eye and said, "I see miracles happening when you play your guitar . . . the mountains will tremble when you lift your voice and sing." It was one of those moments when God spoke kindly to me and confirmed the thoughts and feelings I had inside of me but didn't know how to verbalize. The phrase "the mountains" really captured me, and I wrote it in my lyric book stuffed with scrap bits of paper.

The summer came and I got ready to marry my fiancée, Anna Thatcher. I had bought a two bedroom flat in a small village called East Preston and was fixing it up for the big day when Anna would eventually move in and we'd be man and wife. The church at the time was divided into three congregations, and we met in a school hall in the village every Sunday. One Sunday as we carried Tim's keyboard in, I asked if I could play him a new song. I started singing, *Did you feel the mountains tremble, did you hear the oceans roar?* and a big smile covered his face, followed by a few "woo-hoos" and then a little skip and jump. I finished the song, and we laughed, knowing that God had given us something special for the church and for our youth.

The following week we had our monthly Cutting Edge meeting when all the kids in the area would gather and worship God with abandon. We played the song as a band for the first time, and we must have sung it for 45 minutes as waves of the Holy Spirit flooded that school hall. A generation hungry for God wanted to *open up the doors* and let the world know of this magnificent gospel. Isaiah 54:10 says, "Though the mountains be shaken and the hills be removed, yet my unfailing love for you will not be shaken nor my covenant of peace be removed says the LORD, who has compassion on you."

These were the times when the heavens were opening and nobody knew what was going to happen next. Partly due to not wanting to rush ahead and partly due to inexperience, we would often just wait in silence for 10 minutes, enjoying the amazing presence of God and desperately wanting to hear His voice. There was an army of God being fashioned; and month in and month out, God was birthing visions and dreams, healing wounds, setting us free to dance, asking for our lives. This was the time, this was our time, and we were the revival generation. It was no longer acceptable to keep what we had to ourselves—we were going to let off a holy explosion and take the worship and praise of the saints onto the streets for the ordinary man and woman to hear. We possessed a boldness beyond our years, and we believed that God was truly alive and could heal, save and deliver—whether at the altar on a Sunday morning or in the moments of our everyday lives. *Young and old will turn to Jesus*, we cried, and it was not a youth thing but a church thing, not a denominational thing but a Jesus thing, not a religious movement but a Holy Spirit awakening, and we were all in it together.

The year of Jubilee was the time in ancient Israel when everyone's belongings and land were returned to the original owner and the slate was wiped clean. People were able to start over fresh. What a great symbol of God's people returning to Him and starting afresh, saved and filled with the power of God. Jubilee—starting over under the power of God—is what we experienced, seeing and hearing and feeling the might of the Holy Spirit moving through God's people.

King of
Fools
Stu G

"Sugar and spice and all things nice, that's what little girls are made of."
I've got two girls and no boys, and apart from the obligatory tantrums and
disobedience that every parent experiences from time to time, I have to agree
with that old nursery rhyme! It's been an absolute joy to parent daughters.
They are the light of my life and I would do anything to ensure their wellbeing
and happiness. Soon they'll both be teenagers—and I wait with baited breath
to see if the joy continues!

In our lounge there's a cupboard full of VHS cassettes, not just any old
cassettes, but a catalog of memories from our girls' childhood: *Sesame Street*,
Barbie, Spice Girls, *Cats* the musical, nursery rhymes, sing-a-longs and, of
course, a ton of Walt Disney classics.

On my first visit to the U.S., I was to play as a guest guitarist on a friend's
recording. It was 1996—six weeks before the members of our band were
planning to give up our jobs and pursue the music dream full time. My older
daughter, Kaitlyn, was six years old at the time and a huge Disney fan. *The Little
Mermaid*, *Beauty and the Beast* and *Cinderella* were among her favorite movies.
Not only was I in America, I was in Anaheim, California, the home of Walt
Disney's first theme park—Disneyland!

The recording session was a great success, but I have to say that one of
the highlights for me was my visit to Disneyland. I couldn't believe how the
feelings of childlike, naïve excitement came flooding back. We only had a few
hours there, so we ran around like big kids trying to cram as much fun as we
could into the day. And then came the grand finale: lights, characters in cos-
tume, fireworks and animated projection onto water fountains—brilliant! But
the moment I remember best was when Mrs. Potts (the teapot from *Beauty
and the Beast)* sang to her son, Chip (a tea cup). It was Kaitlyn's favorite song
at that time, and I could hear her little voice singing the tune. I was glad it was
dark—I didn't want my friends to see the tears rolling down my face.

I felt like a fool, but after I thought about it, I didn't care one bit. I started to think about foolishness, and how at times we feel embarrassed and foolish. And then there are times when other people think we're foolish, even when we're convinced that we're doing the right thing.

It must have seemed foolish to some of my friends and relatives to see Karen and me leave secure jobs and a lovely house and move to London to follow a dream. It must have seemed like we were acting out of blind faith in someone we could neither see nor touch, trusting an ancient book and the advice of a few "wacky" friends for guidance on how to live our life.

It's funny how some of the most serious decisions we ever make are easily dismissed as foolish by onlookers. Thankfully things have worked out well for us, and my old friends are pretty amazed at what we're doing now. It's fun to see the look of amazement on their faces when they come to our gigs.

Touring with Delirious?, I get the chance to meet some extraordinary people around the world, people who have heard a call and completely thrown their lives into their dreams—people like Phil Wall. An evangelist, motivational coach, ex-boxer, ex-policeman, amazing husband and father, Phil is an all-round great bloke!

He was on a trip to South Africa a few years ago and was completely blown away by the severity of the AIDS crisis in Africa and the effect it was having on children's lives. He met a young girl called Zodwa, who was an AIDS orphan. Phil and his wife were so taken with her plight that they set about adopting her into their family. The process took over two years, and in the end they were denied permission to adopt her. Of course they were heartbroken.

But the story didn't end there. I think the "never say die" boxing side of Phil came out and he said, "If I can't adopt one, then I'll adopt all of them!" (That's 13 million!) So he set up a charity called Hope HIV. You can get the full story (and make a donation) at www.hopehiv.org.

I remember one event at which Phil did something that was both coura-geous and, from the outside, foolish: the 10/10 Challenge. He re-mortgaged his house, raised about $80,000 and gave $20 to everybody there, with the idea that each person would turn their $20 into $200 and give it back to Hope HIV. How foolish!

But was he really? Listen to how the Word of God weighs in on this matter:

> But God chose the foolish things of the world to shame the wise; God chose the weak things of the world to shame the strong. He chose the lowly things of this world and the despised things—and the things that are not—to nullify the things that are, so that no one may boast before him (1 Cor. 1:27-29).

Simply by saying yes to God and living the life of faith means that some-times we're out there being fools, walking a tightrope in our attempt to live in the world but not be of it. Will we fall or will we reach the other side? Some cheer us to succeed and some hope we'll fail. Think about Peter's water walk (see Matt. 14:28-31). It seems crazy to get out of the boat in the middle of a storm, but if we don't get out, will we spend the rest of our lives wondering what would, could or should have happened?

The life of faith is full of contradictions and paradoxes: *peace and mad-ness, sink or swim, heaven and hell.* The nerve-wracking thing is that we have to work it all out in full view of the world, under the spotlight and in glorious Technicolor. The great thing is that we do not do it alone but with a great King by our side who was crowned with a crown of thorns, falsely accused, jeered and mocked by the crowds. In our journey, we must not forget that our constant companion is *the greatest King of all.*

Majesty

Stu G

I recently heard a talk by Pastor John King of Peoria, Illinois, in which he talked about those moments in your life when you are left with your jaw on the floor, utterly speechless.

He reminded me of how disbelieving most of the world was as we watched the events of 9/11 unfold before our eyes. I can remember exactly where I was: in the kitchen at Furious Records, watching the TV, stunned and unable to believe what I was seeing.

As Pastor John talked of times when he had been in underprivileged communities, my mind was drawn to Delirious?'s time in India, when we had the honor of participating in a program to feed kids in the slums of Hyderabad. Even amid appalling conditions, those kids were so happy with so little—I could not speak as I spooned out the rice on their plates.

I was also reminded of when Martin and I were left speechless at the genocide memorial in Kigali, Rwanda, where 250,000 victims of the 1994 genocide are buried. We stood pondering man's ability to harm his fellow man.

I identified with Pastor John as he spoke about his wedding day, turning around to see his wife walking down the aisle of the church—speechless! And not too many years later as he saw his children born, he experienced that same reaction. I, too, remember that feeling of helplessness and silent awe mixed with joy and the most love I've ever felt!

But he went on to say that there is nothing on this earth that compares with the moment when you are faced with, and encounter, the grace of God, that undeserved love that invites us and enables us to stand in the presence and majesty of God.

I had such an encounter at the end of 2002 in our warehouse.

I'd set up a small demo space so that I could get some writing done for our next album. To be honest, I had not had a great year touring. I'd withdrawn into myself a bit, and I think our gigs suffered because of it. Poor old Martin was out there giving it his all, and he'd look over to me to back him up or go out on some festival ramp for a rock 'n' roll moment, and I was a bit halfhearted in my response. I felt like a fake.

There were a number of reasons for my less-than-inspired performances. My family and I had recently moved into a house and had spent a whole year of evenings renovating, so I was physically worn out. At the same time, we were making *Audio Lessonover* (released as *Touch* in the U.S.), which was a stressful experience, as personalities were not really jelling in the studio. Then a good friend decided to leave his wife, who is also a good friend, and several other close friends were moving away. Now, we artistic types think far too much about this sort of stuff and sometimes end up feeling trapped in our own lives, even though we have the greatest job in the world.

So there I was in my little room, and I just started thanking God for being in control, thanking Him for my life, my family, my band mates, the things we'd seen in our few years together. Before long there was such a presence in the room that I knew I was standing before a King. I was aware that I didn't deserve to be there, but I also knew that the King wanted me there.

I started to write how I was feeling: *Here I am humbled by your majesty, covered by your grace so free, here I am knowing I'm a sinful man covered by the blood of the lamb.* Bible language, I know, but it felt so appropriate. I love the fact that God loves us as we are, no questions asked. A few years ago we played at the Toronto Airport Vineyard, and during our time there someone prophesied to me from the stage. He said, "I don't really know what this means, but I keep hearing the words of this song for you. I think God is saying, 'Don't go changing to try to please me, I love you just the way you are.'"

Back in my demo room, I began to play a few chords and the song started to write itself. *Now I've found the greatest love of all is mine, since You laid down your life, the greatest sacrifice.*

I love the old hymn by Charlotte Elliott "Just as I Am, Without One Plea" with its old-fashioned lyrics—it really describes a genuine grace experience. A couple of verses really stand out to me:

> *Just as I am, without one plea,*
> *But that Thy blood was shed for me,*
> *And that Thou bidst me come to Thee,*
> *O Lamb of God, I come, I come.*

And later:

> *Just as I am, though tossed about*
> *With many a conflict, many a doubt,*
> *fightings and fears within, without,*
> *O Lamb of God, I come, I come.*

Such honesty and understanding is so refreshing—and very much needed. I wanted our new "grace song" to reflect the heart of that hymn. Charlotte wrote that song in 1835, just a few weeks after becoming a Christian, when that feeling of being forgiven was fresh in her experience. I identified with her, having had a similar head-on collision with grace.

I started to think about forgiveness. In the Lord's Prayer, Jesus says, "Forgive us our debts, as we also have forgiven our debtors" (Matt. 6:12). I hadn't realized before that God's forgiving me is linked to how I forgive others! It was a revelation to me, and a truth I try (not always successfully) to put into practice. *Here I am humbled by the love that You give, forgiven so that I can forgive.* I want to spread the joy of forgiveness to those who have offended me!

I gave the song a test drive at church, and the boys were keen to include it on the album *World Service*. Martin and I worked on a few lines together and tweaked the chorus to create what it is today. I really didn't mind if no one liked it or sang it—it was a song for me to sing from the heart. But a few months later, it went to number one on the mp3 guitar rock download chart. So someone must like it!

History Maker

Martin Smith

When Jesus came to Earth as a child, no one could have ever imagined the impact He would have had on His culture and on the lives of billions of people in the ages to come.

The question has been asked, Can anyone really change anything today? Is this it? Do we fit into the system and culture we live in—just see it through till we leave this planet?

The answer we all know is *no*. But still, we're afraid of the challenges and sacrifice involved in being a part of that change.

It's much easier to sit back and let everyone else do it. Jesus proved that it can be done (admittedly it helped a little that He was the Son of God!). But He had to lay His life down at the cross to achieve the most radical change the planet has ever seen or will ever see. He gave humanity the chance to have eternal life—to be set free from sin and our selfishness that separates us from God Himself. He showed us that we don't earn salvation by following a set of rules but by friendship, surrender and commitment to Someone we love.

When we talk about making history, Jesus was the ultimate example of this. Our job is to identify in our culture what needs changing and then make that change, acting as the hands of Christ in whatever situation we find ourselves. It could be sticking up for someone at school whom everyone ridicules, or lobbying government regarding changing laws on pornography.

A friend of mine from Australia, Mark Zschech, is a modern-day history maker because he sees what needs changing and does something about it. In 1994 there was a mass genocide in Rwanda as 800,000 people were killed in a 100-day period, although the rest of world was ignorant of this atrocity. While visiting Rwanda in 2006, he and his wife, Darlene, decided to do something to help the nation still struggling with its own grief. They mobilized their church and thousands around the world to bring hope in that place of despair. For 100 days, foreign doctors taught local doctors how to perform heart surgery; craftsmen built new houses for widows and orphans; musicians sang a new song of deliverance. These people brought about change, real change, stuff you read about in books about heroes of ages past—but this was 2006! The Church was being the Church, showing the love of Jesus.

This ordinary guy with an extraordinary belief in God's ability to do miracles encourages me to believe the same, to think bigger, to believe more, to genuinely believe that we, the Church of Jesus Christ, can change this world. Why? Because His Church is still the most active and passionate people group that exists—and the reason it exists is not for its own gain but to bring light to the world. The Church is an army of volunteers who live for a higher purpose. I love Luke 4:18-19: "The spirit of the Lord is upon me, because he has anointed me to preach good news to the poor. He has sent me to proclaim freedom for the prisoners and recovery of sight for the blind, to release the oppressed, to proclaim the year of the Lord's favor."

I want to be a history maker in this land has been a phrase that many have sung with passion and is one of the older songs (1995) that we still sing every night we play. We joke sometimes that this tune just won't go away! I first wrote the song as the heart cry of a young man with his life in front of him, a prayer to my Maker to use me in whatever way He saw fit. In my mind, I had grand thoughts of wanting to be part of the biggest band in the world.

Life never quite turns out exactly as you'd expect. Ten years into my music career the passion is the same, but I've changed my perspective on what a history maker is. It's not all about the big stuff, about being famous—although that is great. True history makers are those who walk humbly before their God and do whatever He asks. I know many believers who quietly serve God in a radical way, yet they will never receive any recognition. Still, they faithfully see their mission through to the end.

The key is not how fast you run the race but whether or not you finish. I once thought that being a famous band was making history, but now I realize it's more important to be faithful to my wife, to stay married and to see my children become the makers of history in the future. Don't get me wrong—like the song says, I want to be part of changing the course of millions of lives, of seeing the *blind set free* and *dead men rise* and witnessing nations turn back to Jesus. But I'll play whatever part God asks of me.

Each of us is only one small piece of the jigsaw puzzle—and we all must get beyond ourselves to get in God's big picture. Speaking *truth to all mankind* must be our mission, whether on a big or small scale. We must remember that we all have our sphere of influence—we're all part of God's history-making team.

I'm glad this song never goes away, as it reminds us every night what we're here for. I personally have cried many tears in many nations when I've seen people's faces in the crowd light up when they know God is cheering them on. The great cloud of witnesses is watching and waiting, for today is the day. Let's get busy changing the world!

Investigate

Stu G

Guitar players are a strange breed. We like
nothing more than being surrounded by guitars,
amps and tons of pedals and effects to make the
guitar sound . . . well, not like a guitar! We like to talk
about tone, we obsess over whether something sounds better
when using a battery or power supply, and we discuss the benefits
of the latest low-capacitance instrument cable for hours on end.

I've been a customer of Charlie Chandler since 1986. Charlie is one of
the finest guitar repairers and luthiers I've come across. With his brother
Doug, he owned Chandler Guitars in Kew, London, until just a few years
back. That's when Doug moved to the States and Charlie launched out on
his own, continuing to look after some of the finest guitar players in the UK
from his new shop front in Hampton Wick.

Before the album *Glo*, we released *Mezzamorphis*. We had a great experience recording together, and it was a real journey of discovery for me as a
player. I'd admired Lyn Nichols (our Sparrow Records A&R man) as a guitar
player for many years and to get the chance to work with him was fantastic.
Then when we mixed with Jack Joseph Puig at Oceanway studios in Los An-
geles, we were like kids in a sweet shop—all that old gear sounded amazing!

I don't really know why old is good. I guess there was a lot more care
and craftsmanship involved in making guitars and amps 30-plus years ago.

Still, the sounds that forged the music industry years ago are still the sounds we all crave and try to emulate with our mass-produced digital technology.

In 2000, Martin and I were on a visit to Chandlers in Kew, and we spotted an old guitar on the rack. It was a 1937 Dobro single-cone resonator—the sort made famous by the old Blues players like Robert Johnson. We lifted it carefully off the rack and drooled over its subtle tone. It wasn't the easiest guitar to play due to a very chunky neck, but the sound was incredible. I started to pick out some chords in D minor.

Soon we put it back on the rack and left the shop. About a week later I was back in London and received a phone call from Martin. "Stu, go to Chandlers and pick up that Dobro. I've bought it for you—it's got songs in it!" Thanks, Bro!

Back home with my new-old guitar, I started playing around again with those D-minor chords. Nigel Tufnel from Spinal Tap says that D minor is the saddest of all keys. Jack White from the White Stripes says that the D-minor chord has an evil, sad undertone. Beethoven wrote his Ninth Symphony in D minor, and Mozart's Requiem is also in D minor. Whatever your opinion, the fact that one of the greatest guitar solos of all time, Pink Floyd's "Another Brick in the Wall," is in D minor is all the encouragement I need! I just love that key!

I've always enjoyed the psalms; their honesty, truth and raw passion are a constant inspiration. I love how Eugene Peterson, author of *THE MESSAGE*, talks about the psalms.

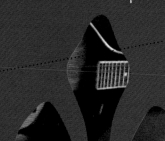

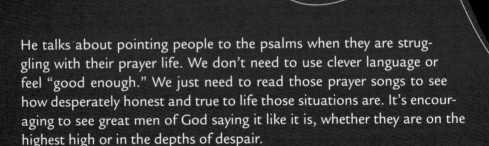

He talks about pointing people to the psalms when they are struggling with their prayer life. We don't need to use clever language or
feel "good enough." We just need to read those prayer songs to see
how desperately honest and true to life those situations are. It's encouraging to see great men of God saying it like it is, whether they are on the
highest high or in the depths of despair.

Psalm 139 is one of my favorites. Whenever I read it, I'm struck by the
words "God, investigate my life; get all the facts first hand" (v. 1, *THE MES-
SAGE*). I really do want to be an "open book" (v. 1, *THE MESSAGE*) and often
think about God exploring my thoughts and motives, searchlight in hand.
Reading this psalm gives me a feeling of being totally surrounded by God—
not being able to escape and not wanting to, either. He knows my thoughts;
He knows the words on my lips before I speak. He is before me and behind
me; there is nowhere I can go to flee from His presence. He formed me and
knew who I was even before I was born. If I could fly away to the ends of the
earth, He'd be there waiting for me. The thing is, I don't feel hemmed in—
I feel liberated.

Psalm 139 closes with the words:

> Investigate my life, O God, find out everything about me; cross-
> examine and test me, get a clear picture of what I'm about;
> See for yourself whether I've done anything wrong—then guide
> me on the road to eternal life (vv. 23-24, *THE MESSAGE*).

Determined words of a psalmist on a journey, flavored with introspection and perhaps a little melancholy . . . perfect for the key of D minor, don't
you think?

Our God
Reigns

Martin Smith

"Our God reigns" is a familiar phrase with anyone who has grown up in church.

There was an old song from the 1970s that we used to sing by the same title, and in those days it was one of a batch of modern-day "choruses," as we used to call them then. I can remember summer camps I'd go on, and a guy with an accordion would lead songs like this. Then we'd all sing along, football-crowd style. What struck me even then is that the great thing about the phrase is that it's an absolute—it's true, it cannot be contested, it's truth with a capital *T*.

When I read that Revelation 19:6 shouts, "Hallelujah! For our Lord God Almighty reigns," it felt like a great time to bring this ancient truth into a modern-day Delirious? song. I remember having had the chorus written for some time and singing one night in my home group with about 20 people there. Everyone sang along, and it immediately felt like it worked.

All I needed was some great catchy church verses and we'd be on our way. I was looking for something easy, not too challenging—and we'd have another church hit on our hands! Then months went by . . . and nothing. I tried every way imaginable to write something, but it just wouldn't come—it was like the pen was angry with me!

I put the song on the shelf and forgot about it for months, wondering whether it would ever see the light of day. Then a very important conversation happened that turned the whole thing on its head. Our friends Matt and Beth Redman were over for a meal, and we got to chatting about the horrific genocide that happened in Rwanda in 1994. To believe that we in the West knew what was going on and yet did virtually nothing disgusted us and made us ashamed of ourselves.

Matt then brought up the issue of abortion and how we know that the lives of millions of babies are extinguished every year and we do nothing about it. We go on with our lives, as though powerless and unaffected. Yet surely abortion is modern-day genocide happening right under our noses. Just because it's culturally acceptable doesn't mean it's right. For example, for years people have smoked in their places of work, but now we know that you will get lung cancer from second-hand smoking. Society has changed its perspective due to the sad reality painted by historical facts. It's now not permissible or cool to smoke in an office with nonsmokers—which gives us hope that maybe on a grander scale that will happen to people's views on the sanctity of unborn life.

I'm not a politician and do not stand in judgment, but in a flash the words started coming, verses full of pain and social dysfunction married to a chorus of truth and adulation. It didn't work on paper, and yet we knew we were on to something.

The song covers three main areas of life that we commonly talk about these days, abortion, HIV/AIDS and cosmetic surgery. There are other equally important subjects but not enough verses!

The first verse puts forward the notion that it's our "right" as a human race to decide the future of unborn children, the notion that freedom comes if we have the freedom to choose. Yet research has shown that our actions have led us to emotional imprisonment, the exact opposite of the freedom we thought choice would bring.

Then the second verse paints an image of twenty-first-century man looking up to heaven and wondering whether this AIDS pandemic will ever pass. It's frightening and alarming to know that the price of a Chinese takeout can pay for antiretroviral drugs that can change someone's life. Have I stopped having takeout? No. Has my heart changed with regard to this issue? Yes. First our head gets enlightened by the knowledge of these things, then our heart begins to experience the pain of it and then ultimately we take our hands down from "worship position number one," and we put them in our pockets to pay the

price for a solution—sometimes with time, sometimes influence, but mostly with our money.

The third verse talks about something less obvious but in some ways more sinister—our obsession with image. No one wants to be boring—and God loves flare, creativity, design and individuality—but we have another problem in our culture and that's the obsession with self. Now again, I don't stand in judgment of anyone as I'm greatly flawed myself in this area, since doing the job I do requires a certain amount of self-care—and that's a good thing to a certain extent. But it's something I've not fully figured out and never will in our world of self-promotion. What is wrong is our cultural obsession with "fixing" ourselves, which springs from the destruction of the family and the absence of real love or affirmation in our lives. In one sense there's nothing wrong with having a nose job, but there's everything wrong about believing it will change how you feel on the inside. Psalm 139 talks about how God knit us together in our mother's womb (see v. 13). He didn't make mistakes when He made us, but our modern world tells us that He did—that lie is to be abhorred.

This song is a celebration of God's love—love for His planet and His people, a chorus of truth amid the confusion of life. The Church at times has kept silent on a lot of social issues, backed away, not rocked the boat, and has subsequently lost its influence. I am a lover of Jesus and His Church and completely believe that *our God reigns*. It's now up to the saints to take the reins back and be world changers for the glory of our God. We can only do it together.

CHAPTER

9

I spread out my hands to you, my soul thirsts for you like a parched land.

Psalm 143:6

It's summertime in West Sussex, England, and the water table below ground is the lowest it's been for years. There has not been enough rain over the last three winters. As a result, we are banned from using garden hoses and sprinklers.

I'm annoyed because I have to fill buckets to wash the car, and the grass has turned brown. My wife, who loves gardening, quietly and patiently gets on with filling the watering can multiple times every evening so that she can tend the hanging baskets and bedding plants—even though it takes five times as long! The result of our different attitudes is that the car doesn't get washed as much and the grass is parched, but the borders and baskets are in full bloom! Patience is indeed a virtue!

The summertime is also festival time. I love festivals, because everyone's in a good mood and excited to hear live music.

Last weekend we played at a festival in the Czech Republic and it was great for a couple of reasons. First, it was our first time in the Czech Republic, and second, it was a mainstream festival headlined by Robert Plant, the legendary singer of Led Zeppelin.

Something amazing happens to us in those environments. It's like we're meant to be there. Let me explain what I mean.

These days we spend most of our time playing Christian events and concerts, and that's awesome, but it's not the whole picture. Back in 1997 we made a decision not to confine our music to the Christian subculture but to take it to the world.

We were encouraging the kids at our concerts to *open up the doors and let the music play*, and we felt it would be hypocritical to encourage others to not imit themselves to their Christian communities and for us to do just that. So we started to release singles into the mainstream charts. I'll never forget the day that "Deeper" made it into the Top 20. More singles, TV appearances and great support tour slots followed. We truly felt alive in those environments, with a clear purpose and a sense of destiny.

At the Ostrava music festival in the Czech Republic, we were amazed to see several hundred Delirious? fans, but they were greatly outnumbered by the thousands of festival attendees who had probably never heard of us and likely weren't interested in the lyrical content of our songs either. Over the years we've worked hard on our performances to make them accessible to every kind of audience. We don't compromise our faith, but we want to rock with the best of them!

While we were playing "Rain Down," I had one of those moments where I was suddenly aware that I was part of something much bigger than just the five of us, you know—that we were made for stuff like this! When we sang the line *I see the clouds and yes I'm ready, to dance upon this barren land. Hope in my hand,* it was like I heard God's voice inside me saying, "This is the barren and I want you to dance on. Don't take these opportunities for granted." I looked out and saw groups of people there for a good time having a beer or two, arms around each other, singing along to the lyrics that were appearing on the screen. We could have spent the whole set prophesying to the crowd, but we got on with singing our songs and winning them over with our music. Something I'll never forget is Martin at the front of the stage in full rock 'n roll pose calling on the Holy Spirit to touch everyone there. I closed my eyes and saw God's love raining down on those people. *Do not shut the heavens but open up our hearts.*

The seeds of "Rain Down" were planted at a festival sound check somewhere in America, when I was messing about with a two-string riff where one string is played open and ringing and the other is played up the fret board. (I was inspired by the latest Placebo album.) It was pretty cool and lasted more than a couple of times round. Jon and Stew started playing along, and before long Martin was singing, *Rain down all around the world we're singing rain down*. This went on for a minute or two, and we had that unspoken, mutual understanding that we had just been given an inspiration for a new song.

Later that day Martin went for a run around the festival site. The sky was growing dark as ominous-looking storm clouds gathered on the horizon. *Looks like tonight the sky is heavy* he jotted down in his notebook when he got back to the tour bus.

We could sense a storm brewing; something changed in the atmosphere. The wind picked up, the air closed in on us and we could see the rain falling in the distance. There was an expectancy that things were about to change. It might have to get a little dangerous first, but ultimately refreshing rain would come.

Whether walking around a festival site in the Czech Republic or in Little-hampton's High Street, one thing I notice is that it's time for change. There is a spiritual famine, but close your eyes and what do you see?

I love the story of Elijah in 1 Kings 18:41-45, a time when there had been a severe famine in the land. Elijah defeats the false gods and then says to the king, "Go eat and drink, for there is the sound of a heavy rain" (v. 41). Elijah goes to the mountain to pray and soon his servant sees a cloud the size of a man's hand on the horizon (see v. 44)!

Can you see the clouds? Can you hear the rain?

CHAPTER 10

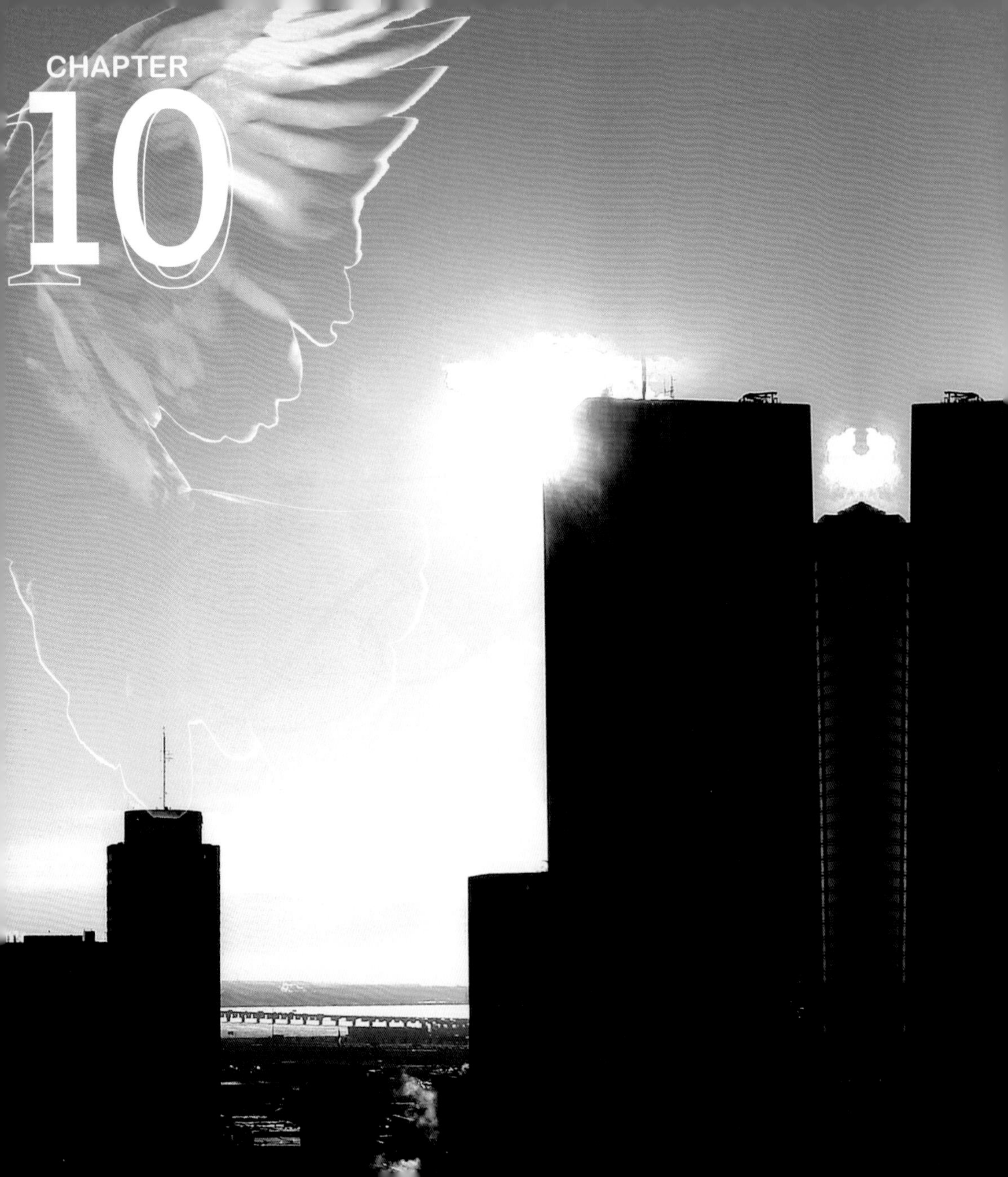

Now Is the Time

Martin Smith

In some ways "now is the time" is an overused phrase. The first time I heard it was used in a forceful way, not brash but with strength and authority.

It was 1995 and a group of emerging leaders from different areas of the British Church were gathering to brainstorm. There was a holy restlessness, a feeling of urgency regarding the state of society and how we as the Church could rise up and be the Bride that Jesus calls us to be.

As part of the gathering, the organizers planned an event they dubbed Remix and invited Delirious? to lead worship for the three-day conference. From the first chord, the whole building shook with the passion of the people, crying out to God to visit our nation and revive His Church. This was the youth of Britain on fire, but among us was an older gentleman, an American from Texas named Dale Gentry. In general we think that to relate to young people we also have to be young and cool, but that's not true. Dale was not young or terribly cool, but we were all captivated by his authority, sincerity and humility, as well as his ability to communicate the timeless voice of God.

"Now is the time, now is the time," he shouted, and his words shot over the crowd like bullets bouncing off the walls. "This is revival generation, now, now, now is the time." The crowd was touched in an amazing way. Some exploded with applause, some sang, some danced, some lay prostrate on the floor, and nearly all wept. God was in the room and He had our attention.

While all this was going on, Jon and Stew kept thumping out grooves relentlessly, and Stu G was weeping through his guitar amp, making noises and melodies that echoed the heart cries of everyone in the room. Tim played signature string sounds that flooded the place like a warm bath after a football match. What was unique about that weekend was the inclusion of DJ Kenny Mitchell in the band, who mesmerized us with his skill, spinning vinyl on the decks, tweaking and bleeping in the same spirit as King David with his harp, holding back the enemy and seeing heaven come. I remember being in awe of what was happening behind me and even more in awe that God was serious about the power of music and that He'd called five ordinary guys from Littlehampton to use it. "Now is the time" rang in my ears for years until 2004 and the recording of *The Mission Bell*.

The winds are blowing through again was always the opening line of the song, but all the lines that followed were constantly being rewritten throughout the recording process. To me this song feels like a "History Maker, Part 2" in its essence—a call to all believers to believe in what we believe in, *a people daring to believe we can change tomorrow*. This great gospel that we love is still relevant today and is our only hope of salvation; but if we're really honest, we have to go beyond preaching that gospel. I mean, what does it really mean to follow God in modern culture? A world awash with materialism and consumerism, post-Christian morals, the destruction of the family, and selfishness that encourages a halfhearted response to God's call on our lives.

It's *time for us to shine*, to stand up and be counted in the towns and cities we live in, to give ourselves to a local body of believers where together we can make a difference. This can never be achieved in isolation but always in unity, when the Church joins hands across its denominational differences and becomes one for the sake of the Great Commission.

There's been a lot of talk in the Christian community about writing more songs about injustice and social issues. Is it possible to write congregational songs about poverty, grief or child trafficking and not spoil everybody's Sunday? Is it possible to highlight some of these issues so that in time they move from our heads to our hearts, and we start to respond to them as Jesus would have done?

I love the image of a city shining on a hill, giving light to all around. Mathew 5:16 says, "Let your light shine before men that they may see your good deeds and praise your father in heaven." That's what the Church does best, more than any other organization in the world, and we must *shine with the face of Christ divine*. During this amazing process of illumination, "our lives gradually become brighter and more beautiful as God enters our lives and we become like him" (2 Cor. 3:18, *THE MESSAGE*). As this happens, we begin to respond to injustice and society's ills by shining the light of Jesus' justice and compassion, battling back the darkness and being *the miracle of light*.

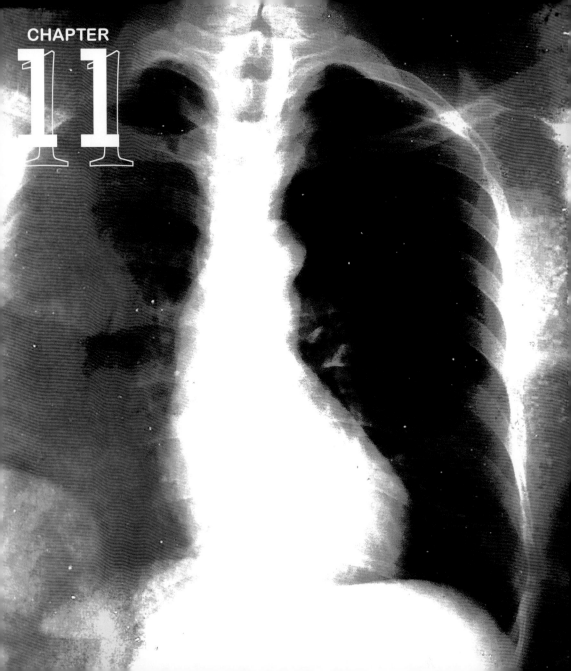

Miracle Maker

Stu G

As I write, my dad is in the hospital. Right now the doctors are performing a biopsy to determine whether a tumor he has is malignant. It is very likely that it's Lymphoma—cancer.

There you are, I said the C word for the first time! I don't know how I feel—I don't know what I think. Even though I left my parents' home more than 20 years ago, Dad's always been there at the end of the phone for advice on how strong to make the mix of sand and cement or to fix something in my kitchen or to discuss the football match or to quite simply be there. I guess things will become clearer after we get the results. For now, I'm praying for a miracle, crossing my fingers and trusting the doctors all at once.

A couple of weeks ago, while Delirious? was on a short tour of the States, my dad e-mailed to tell me he'd been in pain for some time and that his doctor had referred him to a specialist at the hospital. He'd had his first consultation, and they needed to do scans and a biopsy to see what was going on. I e-mailed back saying that we would play the song "Miracle Maker" for him that night.

Flash back to November 2004, Phoenix, Arizona. With the sound check over, Martin and I remained on the stage playing a new chord sequence over and over. Martin said, "Stu, will you remember that?" I said yes, but was thinking, *I hope I can!*

In January 2005, at ICC Studios Eastbourne, in the middle of *The Mission Bell* sessions, Martin said, "I'd love to write a song called 'Miracle Maker.' Can you remember that Phoenix chord sequence?"

I said, "Yeah, I think so," but hoped I could! About an hour later "Miracle Maker" was written and recorded—one of the best moments we've ever had in the studio, a real holy moment, and I still get goose bumps thinking

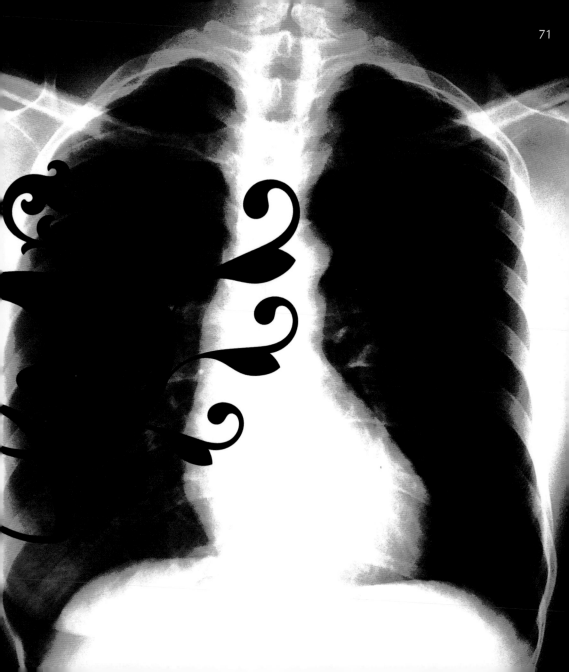

On our minds was the account in John 5:1-15 of the miracle at the pool in Jerusalem called Bethesda. A man who had been crippled for 38 years had been waiting for the angel to stir up the waters day after day, year after year. When the waters moved, whoever got in first was healed of whatever disease he or she had. Amazing!

This man was so infirm, that when this happened, someone else always got in ahead of him. Little did he know that *that* day was the day he would come face to face with the Miracle Maker Himself.

We all need a miracle! Today, I need a miracle for my dad! But there are other miracles: the miracle of salvation, the miracle of forgiveness, the miracle of birth, the miracle of England winning the World Cup? (Just kidding about that last one.) These are all signs of God's breaking through in our day-to-day lives.

This man at the pool had waited for so long, but he hadn't counted on an encounter with the Man who spoke the world into existence.

Yet he does meet Him. Jesus asks, "Do you want to get well?" (John 5:7), and when the man says that he cannot get in the water quickly enough, Jesus tells him, "Pick up your mat and walk" (v. 11). The man was healed and then got in trouble with the religious leaders for carrying his bed on the Sabbath!

When Jesus went to Jerusalem that day, He didn't visit the palaces and royalty but the "hospitals." He went where the people needed Him most. There was a great multitude of sick people waiting for the waters to stir, but Jesus picked out probably the most desperate, the weakest, the most disappointed and maybe the oldest.

Jesus delights to help the helpless!

There's another miracle referred to in the song in the line: *Just one touch is all I need.* This comes from the story of the woman who had been bleeding for 12 years. In Mark 5:25-34 a desperate woman pushed through the crowd to get to Jesus because she knew if only she could touch the hem of His coat, she would be made well! She had spent all her money on physicians but had only gotten sicker. She fought through the mayhem surrounding Jesus, touched His clothes, and the rest is history!

Today, I'm pushing through the crowd and the noise of life for my dad, joining millions of others who are looking for the hand of the Miracle Maker.

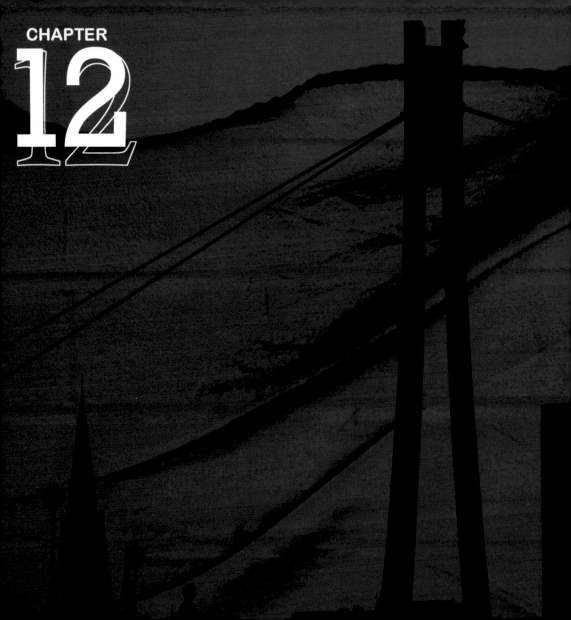

CHAPTER

12

Paint the Town
Red

Martin Smith

was raining hard in the north of England. Tim and I had flown to a small place near Manchester called Clitheroe to spend the day with the famous evangelist Rheinhard Bonnke. It was a small gathering to watch the first stages of the movie he was making about evangelism around the planet.

His passion for God was infectious as he preached to 40 people like he was in the middle of Africa in front of 1.2 million souls. The force of his message blew like a tornado through that village hall, and we were left speechless but stirred into action.

We're going to paint this world red with the blood of Jesus burst from his lips and nearly knocked me off my pew. Like an honest crook, I reached for my notebook and wrote the phrase down, already loving the visual image of the Church going into the streets with the power of God. "'Not by might nor by power, but by my spirit,' says the LORD Almighty" (Zech. 4:6). It was time for the army of God to stand for what it believed in.

During the recording of *The Mission Bell* this concept came back to me on the last day in the studio. I'd been messing about with some musical ideas for a while but it was now or never. I got up early and sat with the acoustic, pen in hand. One by one the guys appeared and started to get a feel for it. We went straight into the live room and cut it in an hour with only 30 percent of the lyrics written. We were all pretty happy, but I knew Stu G was not 100 percent satisfied. He felt the music was a bit wimpy and lightweight for such an aggressive lyrical concept. We agreed to disagree but decided we would revisit it when we could get back in the studio.

Standing in front of Stu G's guitar amps screaming is a little like hearing Mr. Bonnke preach—loud, arresting, passionate, emotional and a lesson in clinical delivery (Stu plays with an accuracy that only a German musician can achieve!). It moves you to want to dance, to sing, to create, to be a rock star, to climb mountains, to open up the windows and let the world hear the sweet tone wafting through the streets like a healing perfume. That day was no exception.

"Mart, I've got a new riff for 'Paint the Town.' I hope you like it." The guitar screamed like an army in battle, and this song had gone from being a teenager to an adult. *Oh, here we come* now sounded authentic as we immediately imagined crowds around the world being inspired to go on a mission, whether in their city streets or the unreached corners of the world. It was "Bonnke meets Blur's 'Song 2'" and we set about finishing the lyrics to the verses.

In a way, this song is different from the normal Delirious? style of lyric: It's rather gung ho in its message. A spiritual testosterone seems to accompany the theme of being *the army of God*. Once when playing in America, a likeable young guy came running up to me, knowing we were about to play and screamed, "Let's give the devil a bloody nose." I don't personally subscribe to this notion, although I understood what he was saying. (It didn't help that he was dressed in camouflage gear and looked like he could remove my head from my body in one quick snap!)

Jesus tells us that we are to take the Kingdom with violence (see Matt. 11:12), and then He also told us to turn the other cheek (see Matt. 5:39). Both notions are correct and true—but it's a paradox. Confused? Don't worry, I am too!

If someone breaks into your house at night and begins to kidnap one of your children, you don't just smile and turn the other cheek, saying in prayerful tones to the criminal, "Jesus loves you and you really shouldn't do that." No, I'd expect our instinct would be to rescue that child at all costs, even at the cost of our life.

Nor did Jesus come to Earth with a spiritual hand grenade in order to wipe out all those who wouldn't follow Him. No, He preaches kindness that leads us to repentance (see Rom. 2:4) and love that leads us to the Creator

of love, God Himself. We need to know we are in a battle—we have been called to rescue our world that is crumbling and drifting farther away from the ways of God. But more than that, I believe we need to be the hands of Jesus to bring love and grace to a generation disenchanted by what can be a hypocritical Christianity, a shallow representation of all Jesus lived and died for.

I'm proud to be in this army, an army that conquers the earth by weeping, mourning and brokenness, a salvation army that is alive and in love with Jesus, ready at all costs to go and *paint this big old town red with the blood of Jesus*.

See you on the front line!

CHAPTER

13

Here I Am,
Send Me

Stu G

My first experience hearing prophecy outside of the Bible or history books was on a weekend in May 1983 when my wife, Karen, and I visited some friends who had a church in London. We'd actually traveled up to the city to see a concert and combined that with a visit with our friends. Neither of us was following God at the time, and we certainly weren't expecting what was about to happen.

We had never experienced anything like it! "Church" to our friends did involve a meeting on Sunday, but it was more about working out life together daily in the hubbub of the city. Constantly busy homes were alive with a buzz, an excitement we'd not experienced before. These people were cool *and* totally on fire for God. They had a purpose for living and a confidence that they were on track and in the right place. If you stop and think about that, it's quite a statement.

So we went to the concert on Saturday and loved it, and on Sunday we went to church. It was held in an old Barclay's bank building on the Hornsey Road in North London. I'd already made up my mind that I wanted to be there. The community's enthusiasm was so infectious! It was okay to belong before we believed.

The folks at the church made Karen and me feel welcome—right at home. Then during the meeting, something happened that changed our lives. We heard someone prophesy. I was stunned that God would speak through a person—not just that, but also use ordinary language to encourage and speak specifically into situations, not clever words alone, but revelation and direction that the prophecy giver could not naturally know about.

That was it for us! We were convinced that God existed and that He was interested in us for who we were, just as we were.

We both gave our lives to Jesus that weekend but didn't say anything to each other for a week or so, just in case either of us didn't approve—it's hilarious when we look back!

Our journey since then has been marked with signposts of "divine appointments" and timely words of encouragement from some amazing people, both in the local church context and while we've been traveling the world. We've been careful not to blindly follow these words but to hold them, test them, be accountable and let God do His stuff in His own time.

First Thessalonians 5:16-22 tells us, "Be cheerful no matter what; pray all the time; thank God no matter what happens. This is the way God wants you who belong to Christ Jesus to live." *THE MESSAGE* phrases it this way: "Don't suppress the Spirit, and don't stifle those who have a word from the Master. On the other hand, don't be gullible. Check out everything, and keep only what's good. Throw out anything tainted with evil."

There were no rock stars in the Bible, but there were prophets—a fantastic collection of personalities, hairstyles, clothes and diets—sometimes putting on an awesome show of God's power and greatness to a whole nation, sometimes simply giving direction to an individual away from the attention of others. One thing they had in common was that they were men and women with a mission, often admired, revered and misunderstood all at the same time. They challenged the rulers and authorities of the day, wanting to bring the nation into line with God's way. I imagine that they were uncomfortable to be around, given their bold ways, and I wouldn't be surprised if they felt uncomfortable with themselves, not feeling as though they fit in with their surroundings or indeed the very skin they found themselves in.

I read a book once by Bishop David Pytches called *Some Said It Thundered*. In the book he documented the stories of several modern-day prophets. Much of the book was about events based in and around Kansas City. Several years after reading the book, Delirious? was invited to take part in a conference put on by Mike Bickle, who is the leader of the church where a lot of these prophets gathered. While we were there, we found ourselves in a room with a guy named Bob—who *had* to see us. I have to say that I was a bit scared. I thought he was going to read me like a book and nail me on my thoughts and "secret sins." He did nothing of the kind! Instead, I was amazed at the look of total acceptance in his eyes and was completely undone.

Then he went round the room and spoke to each member of the band, peeling away the layers of our lives with some amazing knowledge of who we were, even naming our wives and children at times. This certainly got our attention and added weight to what he had to share with us. All these years later, we're still living with and working out what he had to say.

One story he told us was about a young girl who was in his youth group some years previous. She had had a terrible upbringing. Her life had consisted of abuse of all kinds, and she found herself turning to drugs and self-harm to try to take away the pain. Bob and his wife were reaching out to young people like this, constantly giving their lives, love and home to the kids in their group. One day he was reading the account of Saul's conversion on the road to Damascus in Acts 9 and was struck by the thought, *What did Saul see on the road to Damascus? What caused him to fall off his horse and completely turn his life around?* Bob started to pray for the girl that she would simply see a glimpse of what Saul saw and that God would open her eyes.

Jenny had her Damascus Road and is now a key person working with Bob in helping other kids in desperate situations. I'm sure there are thousands of stories like this, but this one got me thinking: All we need is a glimpse!

I started to read about people in the Bible who had a life-changing encounter with God and was really impacted by Isaiah's story in Isaiah 6—his vision of heaven, his feeling of inadequacy, the angel burning his lips and finally God calling him. "Then I heard the voice of the Lord saying, 'Whom shall I send? And who will go for us?'" (Isa. 6:8).

Isaiah's response was, "Here I am, send me!" (v. 8). I was starting to get inspired! I too started to pray for a glimpse: "Show me a vision like Isaiah saw!"

At a gig in Illinois, during a spontaneous moment, I started to sing, "Here I am, send me." The crowd joined in, and at that moment I knew there was probably a song in there somewhere.

Back home and messing around on my Fender Telecaster, I was loving the bite of notes played on a single string and set about creating chord sequences just using a single note each time, not unlike how a string arranger works, layering notes up. It created an "urgent" soundscape to suit the urgency of the lyric, *Show me a vision like Isaiah saw*. There are no standard chord shapes on the recording; they have all been created using single notes.

Life is such a complicated mixture of stuff: work, family, fun and hardship. Chuck it in God's blender and what comes out is what you've got! Regardless of what goes on in life, I want to do my best, and a big part of that, for me, is being ready. When I hear that voice inside asking, "Whom shall I send? And who will go for us?" I want to respond like Isaiah: "Here I am, send me."

CHAPTER

14

August 30th

was still a freelance recording engineer/producer in the early Cutting Edge days and the summer of 1995 was busy with live recordings all over the United Kingdom.

Tim, our keyboardist, had a small studio in Littlehampton, a small seaside town on the south coast of England near where we live. We were privileged to have recorded albums with great people like Matt Redman and Graham Kendrick and by then our own collection of songs.

It was the last weekend in August, and I'd been asked to record the live music at Grapevine, a Bible conference in Lincoln. Anna came with me and we spent a great weekend together. On the last day, we had some brilliant news that Sarah and Stew, our drummer, had given birth to their first child Abigail. We were elated and couldn't wait to get home—just one more meeting to record and we'd pack up and head out.

I can't remember exactly how it happened, but I was asked by the worship leader Chris Bowater to lead one of the songs that night. I was honored and sang "Thank you for saving me." I didn't realize then that these words would take on a new meaning over the next few days.

It was late when we left, but we were excited to get home to see our new little niece. Jon, our bass player, had been at Grapevine too helping with the kids' work and was in the car with us as we set off.

After five hours and only one road from home, I must have relaxed a little too much. I fell asleep at the wheel, crashing the car into a wall. I awoke to the realization that the dashboard was pinning me into my seat; blood was everywhere and I didn't really have a sense of what had happened. Anna and Jon were amazingly okay, but she was running around shouting for help. A paramedic arrived almost instantly, and the process of getting me out of the car began. Firemen, policemen, doctors were all there, helping me to stay calm. Two hours later, after cutting the roof off the car and getting me into

the ambulance, they had me on my way to hospital. The next thing I knew was waking up after having an operation to fix a broken leg and various cuts. For two weeks I was in the hospital, out of action and stuck on my back trying to get better.

I had so many visitors during that time, and my mind started to think about the future. I was grateful to God that I was still in one piece and I knew I'd been rescued. I had been given a second chance and I was going to use it.

One of my visitors was a producer colleague named Les Moir. He brought me a copy of the U2 book *At the End of the World*. I had nothing else to do so I devoured the book, each page captivating and inspiring me. I knew God had my full attention and I knew that we had to go for the music full time. The idea of everyone leaving his job and doing this was scary, as it was historically impossible for a band to earn a living playing Christian music. Yet money seemed like the least of my worries. Besides, when God says "Go," there's no turning back.

I shared my thoughts with each of the guys and everyone was excited but nervous—we were all married except Jon and some had children. It wasn't like we were 17 years old; we were farther down the line and this always makes change harder. We agreed that we would take three months to decide who was going to commit to it and then we'd have three months to wind down our businesses, sell stuff and get ready for our new life. Amazingly everyone jumped in and Delirious? was born. It was a miracle that God had moved us from A to B relatively quickly, and already I could see the car crash had been a blessing in disguise.

We started in earnest traveling Great Britain in our Volkswagen van and a seven-ton truck. I was still on crutches, which must have looked hilarious, and bit by bit we took our music to hundreds of small towns throughout the

UK. When I listen to our music from that period, I can hear a certain frailty in my voice, a thankfulness for being saved, an uncomplicated set of musical prayers. I've also had a physical reminder of that August 30th: Until recently, I've walked with a slight limp . . . and even now, after a long flight, my leg doesn't always work quite right!

With every birthday Abigail has, I remember the goodness of God, first for the gift of her life but also that He saved mine. We as a band never looked back from that moment and have been blessed beyond all measure. It's never been an easy journey, but it's been a fulfilling one. To know "In all things God works for the good of those who love him" (Rom. 8:28) is incredibly liberating, and we have been to many countries around the world, playing in front of many thousands, seeing miracle after miracle.

I will run only for you was the lyrical heartbeat of this song, and a "dangerous" prayer that God has kept us to all these years. I may have a bad leg, but it's pure joy to run this race!

Sanctify

Stu G

April 1, 1996, had finally arrived—the day on which, after six months of discussion, prayer, putting our houses in order and seeking advice, we officially launched Delirious? as our full-time occupations.

We were full of faith and vision. But we were anxious too, wondering, *Can we make it work? Are we good enough? Are we making the right decision?* All we knew was that we had a dream to take our music to the world.

The invitations to play around the UK at different events had been steadily coming in, and Tim figured that if we did three to four gigs a week, our ticket sales, plus selling our cassettes at the back, should provide enough for a small but regular wage.

We were nervous, but along with our wives, had decided to give our lives to this.

It was the second time around for Karen and me. Ten years before, we had sold our house in Ipswich and invested all our money, youthful passion and naïve faith into moving to London, only to get stuck into church and full-time music (but more on that later). We didn't take this second decision lightly. We had two small children, a mortgage, a growing name on the Christian music scene and a growing electrical installation business, but we also had an overwhelming sense that we should do it all over again.

Toward the end of 1996, Martin and I started writing songs together that would become the album *King of Fools*. During that time, I went out for a run one chilly autumn morning around the streets of Rustington in an attempt to keep fit. I noticed I was breathing in a rhythm of every three steps, and I started humming a tune in 6/8 rhythm. I filed this away in my mind to return to later.

Back in the writing room, I could still remember the tune and the 6/8 rhythm and started to work on it. The melody and chords started to form, but the words were a different matter. I was struggling to think of something meaningful, but only ended up with clichéd lines that meant nothing.

Everything had been going so well the past few months and we were on a high. Every week three or four gigs would come and go, incredible times of worship and experiencing God's presence and provision. We were definitely the flavor of the month. I guess that it had been going so well that unknowingly I'd gone into automatic cruise control—knowing how to do the job and deliver the goods. I knew what to say or what notes to play to hit that emotional "God spot"! Looking back, I can see that I'd taken my eyes off the reason for doing what we do, trusting that I could do it without any help. Soon my well had run dry.

I started to pray. So there I was, *in that old place again, down on my face again, crying out.* Hang on, that sounds like a song! But it was more than a song! God was reminding me that it's the humble and not the proud that receive grace (see Jas. 4:6). I found myself crying out, determined to live a different way, not just rely on past experiences but to keep pushing in and pressing on.

I'm sure I felt God smile. I started to think about the word "sanctify" and didn't really know what it meant. So I did some research. (Now I just want to say that I am not a theologian—I play guitar in a rock band! But often in conferences and seminars, we find ourselves having to explain our songs and thoughts.)

Sanctify. I want to be set apart right to the very heart. The definition of "sanctify" is "to set apart or make holy." But how do I do that?

I discovered that 1 Thessalonians says:

> May God himself, the God of peace, sanctify you through and through. May your whole spirit, soul and body be kept blameless at the coming of our Lord Jesus Christ (5:23).

This is a difficult task, keeping ourselves set apart for the Lord. It's so easy to give your heart away. Let me explain what I mean by this. As very young Christians, Karen and I lived and worked with our pastor. He was a brilliant and gifted man, and I ended up living on every word he said and relying on him to make decisions for me. I'd given him a place in my life that really should only belong to God. Of course I didn't find out until he made a terrible mistake and it all went wrong—and I was sent reeling! My foundations had been in the wrong place. First Peter 3:15 tells us, "But sanctify Christ as Lord in your hearts, always being ready to make a defense to everyone who asks you to give an account for the hope that is in you" (*NASB*).

That was another "on my knees" moment, when I gave my life back to my Creator.

Today I'm determined to live my life differently, not hiding away from the world, but not getting sucked in either. I want to taste the fruit of those times on my knees and continually find myself on my prayer mat, not because I'm desperate and empty, but because I want to be continually plugged in to God's power grid.

How long will it take? How long will I have to wait? God knows us intimately inside and out. He looks at the heart and not the circumstance. I mess up, and He is bigger than my mistake. I succeed and He is bigger than my success.

The life of faith requires all of our mind, soul, strengths, gifts, abilities, money and more on a daily basis. But without the power and presence of God, our offerings are pointless.

> *Lifted up I've climbed with the strength I have*
> *Right to this mountain top*
> *Looking out the cloud's getting bigger now*
> *It's time to get ready now!*

CHAPTER

16

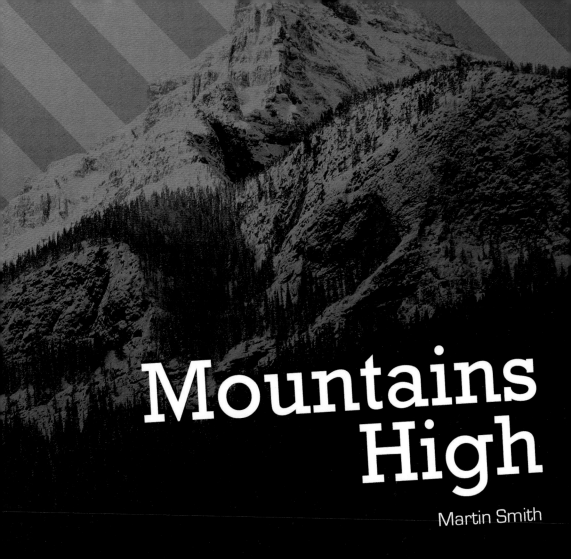

Mountains High

Martin Smith

on's dad, David, is also the pastor of our church, Arun Community Church, and we meet in the senior school in Littlehampton on the south coast of England

In December 2002, Jon's uncle, John, was also on the leadership team, a great man of God, married to Jo; he and his wife were the parents of teenaged girls. He was preaching in Switzerland and on his morning off went up the nearby mountain to go skiing with friends.

Tragically, it was on that mountain that he died.

The phone rang in our kitchen at about 6:00 P.M. that night. And you know how sometimes you can tell by the way it rings whether it brings good or bad news? Well, that day the ring had an eeriness to it, and we somehow knew something was wrong. "John died," the voice shrieked. "A heart attack killed him."

Anna put the phone down and repeated the news in a state of calmly spoken shock. Then there was silence and the room filled with disbelief. *John can't die; he's only 44. He's a great man doing God's work—this can't be true.* Our minds were full of questions as to why our God would allow this.

That night went painfully slow. It was an effort to do anything, and we were walking around in a trancelike state, still no tears but an incredible weight of sadness. We eventually put the children to bed and came downstairs to a feeling of emptiness. For some reason, when there is grief your instinct is to reach out to a higher being, a higher force that can explain the reason for your loss. I went to the piano, lit a candle and sung the line *Sorrow came to visit us today*. The words came with a fragility I had not experienced before, haunting holy words in small waves, like the breath of a sleeping baby.

Sometimes you craft a song for the sole reason that you want people to be able to identify with it and sing it in church on a Sunday morning. There were no such thoughts that evening—just a grieving soul sitting at a piano, pouring but what was inside of me—questions with no answers, loneliness, confusion, loss and shock. Emotions I'm sure we've all experienced at some time.

Here I was grieving for Jo and the girls, not knowing how we were going to get over it, how we were to move on. *This mountain's high, too high for us* became the chorus, and I loved it for its honesty. The song continues, *through God we can overcome all things.* I believed it that night, and I believe it now—but that's not how I *felt* and it's okay to put that emotion into songs. There is a mystery to God and this life we live here on Earth. God does not tie up all the loose ends for us. If life here were perfect, there would be no need for a Savior.

It's not wrong to write God songs that don't provide all the answers—we have a thousand songs that do that. But very few psalmic songs are allowed to express the raw emotions and the very real questions that spring from living life in a world where pain hurts. For some reason we as Christians are afraid to lament. Our modern theology calls for a certain kind of "stiff upper lip" mentality.

Jesus came so that we could be victorious and that's completely true. But often life brings sorrow, and it's okay in the short term to feel like the rug has been pulled from under our feet. We must remember that God created us humans with all these complex emotions—we are not robots that soldier on regardless. To deny our emotional life can be damaging to ourselves and to the people around us.

Time has moved on and Jo and the girls have been "victorious." They did get over the mountain they thought they would never climb, and they held on to God in the most extraordinary way. They had felt abandoned by God but in the very same moments knew the extravagance of His love. Rachel, Susannah, Naomi, Elisabeth and Mum, this song is for you, because you have shown us all with pride and dignity, with strength and determination, how to follow

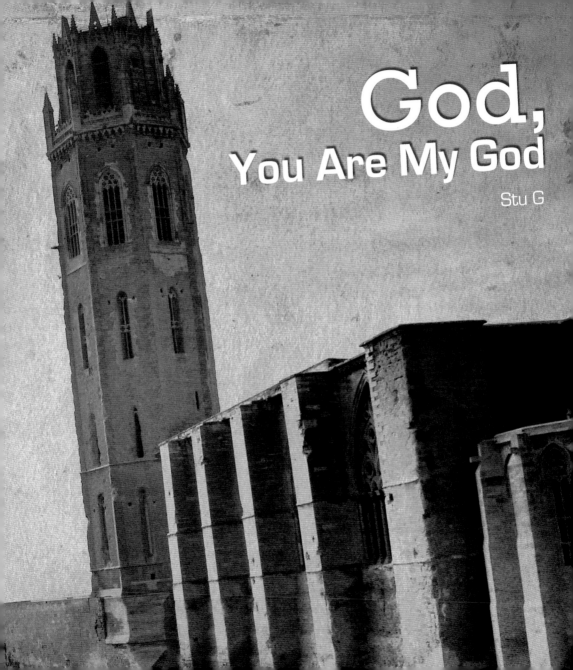

God,
You Are My God

Stu G

I love the psalms. I love Cathedrals. I love vegetable gardens . . .

I love the *psalms*. The highs, the lows, in the place of plenty, in the desert, quiet reflection, raucous praise, honesty, questioning, real-life issues, gut-wrenching faith—it's all there.

"God, You Are My God" is taken from the first five verses of Psalm 63. This is a psalm of King David (see v. 11) and was probably written when he was in the desert fleeing his own son Absalom, who wanted to be king and had "stolen" the hearts of the men of Israel (see 2 Sam. 15:6). What I find interesting is that although King David is fleeing to the desert, the first thing he does is to go to the mountain and worship God.

I wrote "God, You Are My God" in the early nineties, just before I met up with the rest of the guys at Cutting Edge. I was a full-time worship leader for the Praise Community Churches in the East Midlands and had a fantastic time there. It was a real discovery time for me—in at the deep end but trusted by the people. We discovered a lot together about the presence of God. I remember often going into our meeting room the morning after a worship service and sitting in the presence of God, still tangible from the night before. I'd just sit there, think and pray.

I was reading Psalm 63 one day when the opening lines struck a chord with me. I wanted to write lines of simple truth that are repetitive—and so get inside your head, not unlike some of the liturgy that the Church of England and the Catholic Church use. These forms of worship are so easy to remember and very useful when you find yourself in difficult situations, because if you commit this stuff to memory, it'll be there somewhere on your brain's hard drive. It's useful to speak truth, even if you don't feel like it. After all, truth is truth no matter how we feel or where we find ourselves.

I love *cathedrals*. In the UK some of the buildings have been there since Anglo-Saxon times—for hundreds of years people have gone to these places to seek God. The pilgrims' passionate search and honest prayers have soaked into the very stones and have left behind an intense atmosphere. I hope they found what they were looking for!

Cathedrals give me goose bumps. Cathedrals make me cry. One of my lasting memories of cathedrals is when I was playing guitar for Ben Okafor, a Nigerian reggae artist (and let me just add that playing for Ben was always fantastic). Anyway, we booked for an all-night festival that was held at Lichfield Cathedral.

It was awesome! The gig was great but being awake all night in such a place was what impacted me most. I wandered around, senses heightened by the fact it was dark and in the middle of the night. As the music grew faint in the background, I found a painting on the wall that depicted a monk writing—and the painting was dated from the fourteenth century, so it had been there over 600 years! There had been a place of worship there as far back as the seventh century. I sat in the choir stalls and was joined by a bishop who answered all my questions regarding the history of the place and about how Christianity found its way to the UK. I had found a place of prayer dating back farther than the cathedral building itself! I lit a candle and sat there for a while in silence.

Another inspiring cathedral moment was in 2004 when Karen and I were on a weekend break to Barcelona. (A side note: It's a great city, so if you ever get the chance to go, well, go!) We fell in love with the place and were stunned by the buildings of Gaudi. We walked for miles searching out these extraordinary and beautiful buildings. He certainly left his mark! The building that stunned us the most was The Temple de la Sagrada Familia. Visible from around the city, this cathedral fulfilled Gaudi's vision to create a building where people would look at it and praise God. He succeeded!

Even after his death, the cathedral is not finished yet is still being built according to his plans. (Sound familiar?) Parts of it are a hundred years old and some parts are brand new. I find it amazing that Gaudi's design for the supports of the structure are based on nature, and in particular, trees. He shocked the architectural world when it was discovered that this design was strong and safe enough to hold up the enormous weight of the building. The towers are a mark of not just the building but also the city. These "Towers of Praise" rise up to the sky with words like *Hosanna* and *Excelsis* emblazoned on the sides, spiraling heavenward.

It is experiences like these that inspired us to record a choir of monks as the opening to our album *Glo*. But where did we find them? After some searching, our manager, Tony Patoto, discovered the monks of Ampleforth Abbey. We managed to track down Father Oswald, who was in charge of the choir, and asked if they sang Psalm 63. He said that they sang over 30 versions, English, Latin, happy or sad, and which would we like? They were even up for singing *our* melody or their versions in our key.

Tim and Paul Burton, our infamous sound engineer, traveled to Yorkshire and had a very full day recording a dozen monks singing Psalm 63 in all manner of ways, complete with a few lines from our version of the song.

They were really impressed by abbey life and the monks' devotion to a different way of life. And that brings us to . . .

Vegetable gardens. I love vegetable gardens. On holiday this year in France, we walked past a cute little cottage. It had a large front garden, the whole of which had been turned into a vegetable garden. There were neat rows of plants, some ready to harvest and some continuing to grow, with not a weed in sight. I couldn't forget it. It seemed to speak to me of a different way of life.

Here in France the pace of life is a little slower anyway, but it was the gardener's devotion and diligence that really got me. To take care of it meant that he had to tend it every day, watering the plants, removing the weeds, picking the crops. He has a beautiful way of life, spending his time taking care of the things that really matter to him.

My life is so full of deadlines, e-mails, phone calls, airports that sometimes it's easy to forget to take care of the things that really matter: my devotion to God, my devotion to my family. I can appear to say or even do the right things, but often I'm distracted.

I'm still living in Psalm 63 after all these years—seeking God, searching for His power and glory, like a desert wanderer seeks water. I'm looking for a way to get everything done but, at the same time, live a life of devotion—a life that leaves my soul satisfied.

I'll let you know if I find it!

CHAPTER

18

I'll See You
When I Get There

Martin Smith

3016LA-983509

HIGH PO

7951 5

It was the first of the month and April Fool's Day. Our children had hardly slept a wink because we were heading to America for the annual Delirious? family tour. They could hardly contain their excitement at being on the tour bus with Dad, traveling across the United States. It was 1994 and our four children were also happy for another reason: Their mum was expecting another baby and they were going to have another little sister or brother. (It's fantastic seeing your own kids excited about a new arrival.)

As I awoke that morning, I could hear sobbing coming from the bathroom. It was my wife, Anna, and I knew something had to be wrong. Those who know Anna know that she is always radiant, but on that day she was pale, with fear in her eyes. "Mart, I've been bleeding all night, and I'm so scared we're going to lose this baby." Fear came rushing in as two years before we had also had complications with our fourth child, Levi, when at a 20-week scan, we were informed that he might not survive. But by the grace of God he came into the world healthy and happy, and you wouldn't know anything was amiss if you saw him now, wrestling with his older brother. But it was a gut-wrenching time as we were taught a lesson about the fragility of life.

Here we were again. We cried, hugged and prayed without speaking a word—there weren't any consoling things to say, just a sense of numbness and unknowing. We had no choice but to get dressed, be excited for the other children and get to the bus on time to take us to the airport. It was too late to back out, and we asked God to carry us through the day.

Any of you who have traveled with kids or been on an airplane with a little one kicking the back of your chair will understand the stress of taking kids into small places where they have to sit still for 10 hours—it's not normal! Any hopes of maintaining the air of a cool rock star go out the window as bags, milk bottles, strollers and overexcited children hang from arms and legs. It's fantastic and challenging all at the same time but having them with me

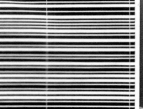

Smith / Martin

3016UA-983509

HEAVEN / HIGH PO
HVN 76515
IAD 9252

3016UA-983509
Smith / Martin
16UA-983509 HVN

when I travel is a big reward and makes me the happiest guy in the world.

Everyone was upbeat and all five families were traveling together, ready to hit the road for another 20 dates in front of American crowds. Quietly, Anna and I were still fearful, praying and hoping things were going to be okay. But sometimes things aren't always okay, and to cut a long story short, we lost our baby during that flight. At the time I remember we just held hands—there was no escape from this nightmare. All we wanted to do was land in Chicago and go straight back home. Going home was our natural instinct, but life isn't always that simple or convenient. We had four other children excited, dreaming about having the time of their lives, 20 concerts with thousands of people waiting, and financial responsibilities toward my band mates. With all of this in mind, Anna convinced me that we should keep going.

The next day was Elle's birthday (our eldest daughter) and the first gig. As we all crowded around the birthday cake, we sang "Happy Birthday," and in my heart I thanked God for her life, for the gift she is to us. Often in life you just have to carry on.

I remember the gig that night so vividly, singing "History Maker" and "Mountains High," full of emotion as every line passed by. We encored with "Investigate," which is based on the theme of Psalm 139. As I sang the words, tears flowed as a sense of sadness and hollowness came on me. When you are in a band for so long, you feel each others' emotions like their your own, and I knew Stu G was playing his screaming guitar solo for us. The last note came and then huge applause; I walked to the monitor board and Jon took me in his arms like a little baby and I cried for home. It's a gift from God to have friends and an even greater gift to have brothers and confidantes.

God's grace was with us, and we saw Him do amazing things on that tour. It taught me that it's always good to keep singing God songs in the middle of times like this because they put life in perspective. We can better relate to the pain and sacrifice Jesus went through to bring us the gift of salvation.

One of those nights on the tour bus, I scribbled in my notebook some thoughts about meeting this baby whom we lost here but will meet in heaven one day. I had this picture of him or her meeting Anna and me at the gates of heaven and taking us to see Jesus, along with our other children. I remember the feeling of joy at meeting my unborn child and my heavenly Father—a sense of pure ecstasy that we had made it home and would be together forever.

I've had so many letters about this song, "I'll See You When I Get There," from people who have lost loved ones and who have taken comfort from these words. It's already been played at many funerals and I'm glad it made the record, although it was an odd fit in some ways.

We can never figure out in this life exactly what God's doing—especially when we're living through painful experiences. But we do have to trust that God is in control. Just a year later, there were tears again—but this time they were tears of joy as we huddled round the hospital bed to meet Ruby-Anna

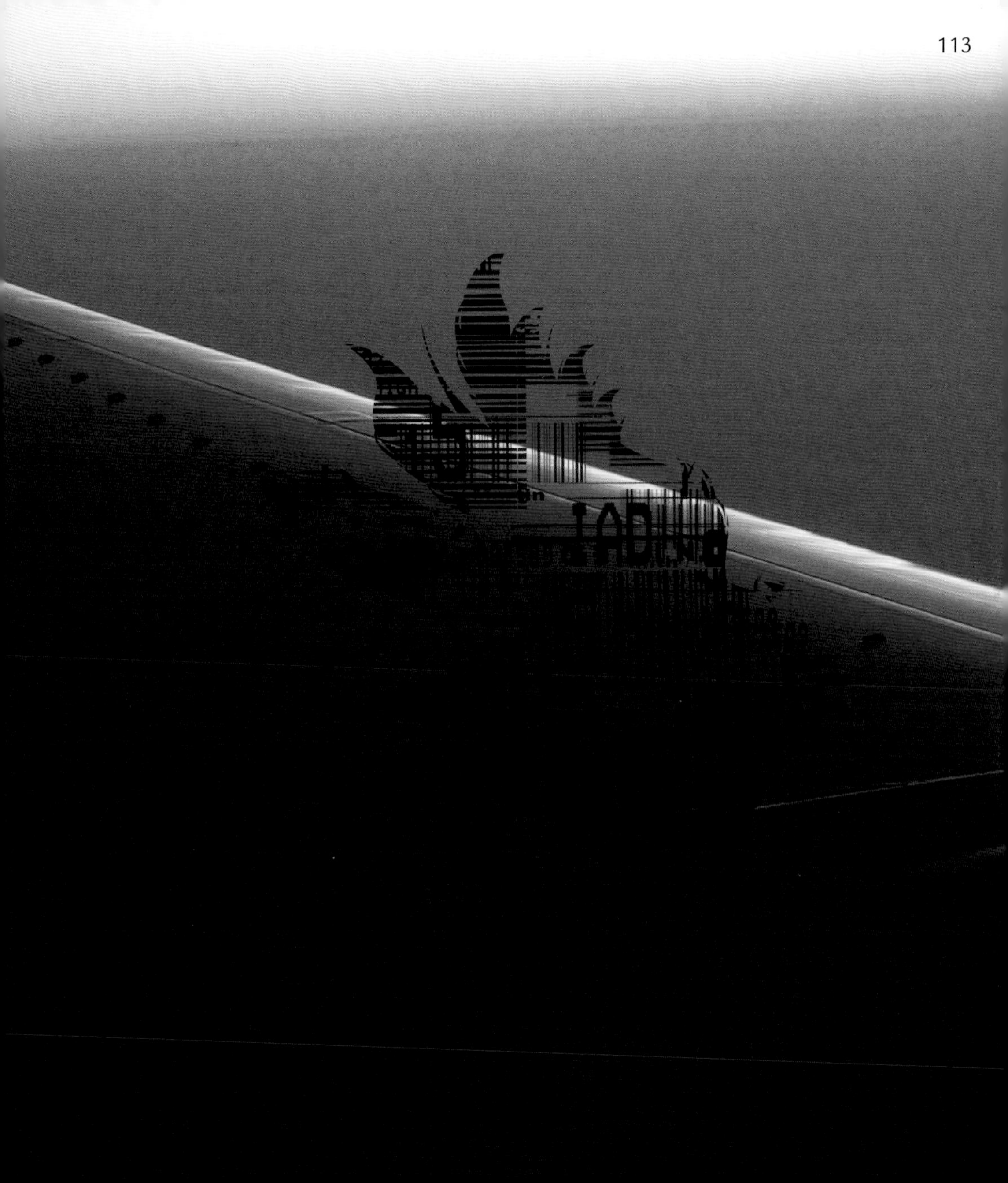

Lord,
You Have My Heart

Martin Smith

This story begins in 1989, when this song was written on the back of a napkin stained with tomato ketchup. Life was about to change, but I didn't for one moment conceive how much as I stepped aboard God's great roller coaster. For the first time in my life, Christianity had gone from my head to my heart and this great journey had begun. The words flowed from a chewed-up pen and the first love song to my Savior had surfaced in a natural and uncontrived way, simply saying, *take my life and use it.*

I had prayed this prayer on numerous occasions, being brought up in a churchgoing household with Christian parents. This prayer first came from the lips of my parents when at my birth I nearly died of bronchial pneumonia, spending the first six months of my life not crying or making a noise—and lying in an "iron lung" to help my lungs breathe. My mum and dad cried out that I would make a sound and offered me back to God in return for their son's life.

Since I hadn't cried since the day I was born, they prayed that God would heal my lungs and give me a voice. I survived and have somehow always lived with a sense of thankfulness. The next time was at the grand old age of 8, when I gave my life to Jesus. Yes, I was very young but knew that I was doing what I needed and wanted to do—and at the age of 12, I went on to be baptized.

Soon I was 13 and we had to move due to my dad's job. I ended up in a school in Surrey called Wallington High School for Boys, where I threw myself into sport after sport. The church we attended near our new home had no real youth group, so my dad started one. And there was no one to lead the singing, so dad asked if I'd learn guitar. I remember him picking me up from a cricket game and taking me to the local music shop. An hour later I was the proud owner of a beautiful electro-acoustic guitar!

So with guitar in hand and a chord book, the songs started coming— first composing deep love songs about my 13-year-old girlfriends and just enough time to learn a church song for the youth group to sing! I had found something I loved and gave all my spare time to it, so much so that my mum had to lock it in the garage for a week so I'd do my homework. Subconsciously the "take my life" prayer was going up to heaven again, although I had no idea then that God would keep me to it.

The summer of 1989 had arrived and I was hungry for God. I was 19 years old and working as a sound engineer for a recording studio in Eastbourne called ICC. As well as working with local bands, part of my job was to record all the music at Bible conferences around the country and compile live albums of the worship times. One of these worship gatherings was New Wine, which was held in the west country of England. As I sat with headphones on, in the middle of the hall, surrounded by 5,000 people singing to God like I'd never heard before, I realized that somehow these people had more than I did. But I couldn't figure it out. I'd been to church all my life, knew all that there was to know, and yet these faces were radiant with love for their God. Something was happening to me, and I knew I needed what they had but didn't know how to get it!

At the end of the week I knew I needed to be filled with the power of God, just like the disciples were (see Acts 2). I needed my relationship with God to go from being just cerebral to emotional and experiential. I wanted to know my heavenly Father intimately and to be a friend of God who daily walked and talked with Him. On the last night someone asked if he could pray for me, so there I stood with my headphones on, arms open, saying once again, "take my life and use it." Nothing really happened. I mean, I wish I could recount that lightning bolts came from the sky and smoke surrounded me in a holy haze but, alas, nothing of that sort. However, I knew something had changed, and I went to bed that night with a strange sense of peace and excitement rolled into one, not knowing that the next day I would write my first ever song of worship.

I remember that afternoon sitting on my own in this empty hall with a borrowed guitar, not trying to write a worship song, but just putting my prayer to music: *Lord, you have my heart, and I will search for yours. Jesus, take my life and lead me on.*

There was the prayer again, the same one my parents had prayed all those years before, as they dedicated me back to God. I wasn't a child any longer and knew the seriousness of the call. I knew that I was giving my life to God for Him to use; it was time to be a "living sacrifice" (Rom. 12:1) and to live a life that pleased my God and made Him smile.

We'll see your glory here has been a lyrical theme that has surfaced many times in our songs throughout the years and has been a mandate for the band through the twists and turns of our journey. Lord, for Your glory, *take this life and use it.*

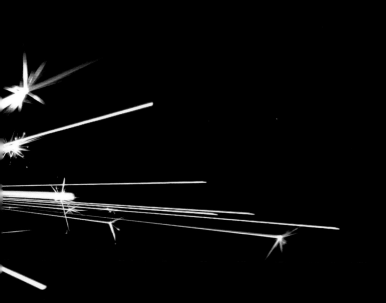

See the Star

Stu G

When we're journeying with God, He'll take us where we need to go. And this is no small thing, because in life it matters to most of us where we are going. Consider this passage from *Alice in Wonderland*:

> "Would you tell me. . . which way I ought to go from here?"
> "That depends a good deal on where you want to get to,"
> said the Cat.
> "I don't much care where—" said Alice.
> "Then it doesn't matter which way you go," said the Cat.

It's a cliché, but life *is* a journey and it *does matter* where we're going!

I do not have all the answers, and I wrestle with questions and tussle with challenges on a personal level. I take deviations and rabbit trails, but I always want to have my eyes on the finish line and not look back. Paul the apostle put it like this:

> Brothers, I do not regard myself as having laid hold of it yet; but one thing I do: forgetting what lies behind and reaching forward to what lies ahead, I press on toward the goal for the prize of the upward call of God in Christ Jesus (Phil. 3:13-14, *NASB*).

The Delirious? journey has been an amazing experience so far. The vision has been, and still is, to make great music and to help people discover more about God. Our eyes are fixed on that—that's never changed. The steps and goals along the way are the things that have shifted and have taken us along some interesting roads. From releasing chart singles to performing at a Joyce Meyer crusade, we see it all as part of the picture.

Something that has marked our journey from day one is that we are not alone. For a start, there are five of us in the band, and along with Tony (our manager until 2005), we've had each other as team members in the race. I'm also humbled by the fact that our journey has been joined by thousands of others who come to the gigs, are into the music, visit our website, have caught the vision and who also feel part of the team.

Then there are those who've gone before us. I'm often aware that we're being cheered on from afar, as it says in Hebrews 12:1:

> Therefore, since we are surrounded by such a great cloud of witnesses, let us throw off everything that hinders and the sin that so easily entangles, and let us run with perseverance the race marked out for us.

In the early days of Cutting Edge, we used to travel to our friend Billy Kennedy's church in Southampton. The church building is the old Methodist Central Hall and was built in 1925, the site where Welsh revivalists George and Steven Jeffreys held some meetings, bringing a great number of people to God. Inside the hall I was always aware of the "great cloud of witnesses." Wherever you stood, you were surrounded on all sides by the old original pews and you could just imagine those faithful saints cheering us on. It was a great atmosphere to play in, and we'll never forget one night seeing a young girl freed from her wheelchair, able to walk (and she's still walking today!).

We're also joined on our journey by our church. We really love our church! It's not the best, biggest or most mind-blowing church in the world, but it's full of amazing people. One such person is a lady called Jo who, together with her husband, John, have been key leaders. John and Jo have constantly urged us on

One Sunday morning, I could see Jo was having some sort of God encounter. She made her way to the front and started singing into the microphone: *See the star that's breaking through to shine upon the people of promise.* Over and over again, in a shaky voice, she repeated the phrase. I don't know why, but it's one of the strongest memories I have of our church. I can't forget it and can still see the picture it painted in my mind: thousands of people on a journey, eyes fixed on their destination bathed in light.

I went away and started writing "See the Star."

So we run never stop keep my feet on the road. I wanted to portray that determination to never give up, to keep going no matter what. That's easy to say when life is going well. *But what ya gonna do when the walls come down and fall on you?*

Jo has had to deal with the harsh reality of this. In 2003 her husband, John, had a heart attack and died while on a ministry trip to Switzerland. Talk about the walls crashing down! Three years later and I see a woman who has never stopped running, has kept pressing in, has kept living the life and dreaming the dream. She has reached a place in prayer that as yet I haven't experienced—and when she speaks, we listen. Keep going, Jo, there's more to come! "See the Star" was our first single off *Mezzamorphis*, and there are differing opinions regarding whether this was the right choice or not. But the fact is that this song captured something about where we were at on our journey and still rings true today.

My wife and I have just started helping run a cell group for older youth in our church. It's not a youth group and we're not youth workers! The guys and girls are 18 to 21 years old—old enough to vote, drink in a pub and get married. They have been through school and college and are ready to take on the world! We really love them and, what's more, believe in them—and if there's anything we can do to help them figure life out, we'll do our best to do it. Some of them have real ambitions and know where they want to go, while others need a bit of help working it all through.

At this point in our journey, it's time to pass on the things we've learned. We're saying, This is where we are at now, this is what we've learned so far, we've got a long way to go, but we're persevering to the end—do you want to come with us?

Two thousand years ago, wise men followed a star. In Revelation 22:16, Jesus calls Himself "the bright Morning Star." In the Gospel of John, Jesus calls Himself "the light of the world" (John 8:12).

Maybe wise men *do* still follow a Star.

Also Available in the Best-Selling Worship Series

The Unquenchable Worshipper
Coming Back to the Heart of Worship
Matt Redman
ISBN 978.08307.29135

The Heart of Worship Files
Featuring Contributions from Some of Today's
Most Experienced Lead Worshippers
Matt Redman, General Editor
ISBN 978.08307.32616

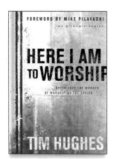

Here I Am to Worship
Never Lose the Wonder of Worshiping the Savior
Tim Hughes
ISBN 978.08307.33224

Facedown
When You Face Up to God's Glory, You Find
Yourself Facedown in Worship
Matt Redman
ISBN 978.08307.32463

Available at Bookstores Everywhere!

Visit **www.regalbooks.com** to join **Regal's FREE e-newsletter.** You'll get useful
excerpts from our newest releases and **special access to online chats with
your favorite authors.** Sign up today!

Regal
God's Word for Your World™
www.regalbooks.com